戊
戌
年

The Year of the Earth Dog

Chinese Astrology for 2018

JOEY YAP RESEARCH GROUP SDN BHD (944330-D)
19-3, The Boulevard, Mid Valley City,
59200 Kuala Lumpur, Malaysia.
Tel : +603-2284 8080
Fax : +603-2284 1218
Email : info@masteryacademy.com
Website : www.masteryacademy.com

CHINESE ASTROLOGY

ASTROLOGY

FOR

2018

戊戌

狗年運程上卷

THE YEAR OF THE EARTH DOG

INDEX

3. Personalised Forecast for 2018 based
   on Day of Birth   107
(Assessment based on the 60 Jia Zi 甲子 Day Pillars)

PREFACE

The Chinese Astrology is a profound and interesting area of Chinese Metaphysics, also tagged as the popular guide to the prospects of the year. 'Astrology by animal sign' is a simplified form of astrology reading, adopting the sole view of one's Earthly Branch from his or her BaZi. In view of the straightforwardness of this method, it offers the most simplistic view of one's annual outlook.

Anybody with a clear insight into BaZi studies knows that it would take all the Eight Characters (the literal translation of the word "BaZi") to obtain a full and comprehensive forecast or reading. By looking at only one aspect of the Earthly Branch of the Year Pillar, the readings are at best inconclusive and because of that and it is estimated to only amount to 12.5% in accuracy. Hence, here comes the importance of "looking at the bigger picture". A comprehensive BaZi assessment, which includes all of the four Pillars on the Earthly Branches of one's BaZi Chart, gives you different insights into different aspects of your life, providing you with a stronger and more cohesive understanding of your annual forecast.

Although it is laced with certain limitations, the 'Astrology by animal sign' still proves to be a very useful analysis, and the go-to method for many to obtain some form of proper astrology information based on the real stars used in Chinese Astrology and Metaphysics. Unlike other astrology books in the market that provide generic characteristics of animal signs in a sugar-coated and entertainment-driven manner, the book you are holding not only compiles and presents direct information for the outlook of the Twelve Animal signs for the year and month, it also opens up the personalised outlook for the Year of the Earth Dog based on your Personal Day Pillar *Jia Zi* (甲子).

To put it in another way, this book aims to impart and clarify a set of more accurate and relevant information – information we really need and want to know in order to strengthen your comprehension and give you something precise to get you going for the year.

So, treat this book as your map and compass to get your bearing for the next twelve months. Poring through this book will give you a rough idea on what to expect for the year, and grant you the needed access for you to embark on the necessary remedial actions or the right course of response to change the path of your life in general. At times, the road to your destiny may not be altered easily, but you could certainly put your own personalised touch to smoothen the destination. Keep this idea in your mind and you will notice how big of a difference it would make!

In Chinese Metaphysics and Astrology, your luck is divided into Man Luck, Earth Luck and Heaven Luck. Hence, nothing is ever "wholly good" or "wholly bad". For instance, a less than stellar forecast does not spell a completely doomed year for you. Instead, view that resistance as your motivation to strive harder to affect change. By doing so, you will get to see positive improvements and ensure that the year's inauspicious luck is minimised. At the end of the day, you are only scratching the surface if you rely solely on the "good" or "negative" forecast given. Your set of actions, responses and initiatives certainly pen a louder and more significant forecast than the one written here.

Despite it all, I need to remind you that the information in this book constitutes only a small percentage of your BaZi and Destiny Chart analysis. The only way to gain insights into the specific appreciation of what the Year of the Earth Dog holds for you is to have a professional astrology consultation using either the Purple Star Astrology (紫微斗數 Zi Wei Dou Shu) or the BaZi Four Pillars method.

Having said all that, I hope you will find this book practical, useful and most importantly, informative enough to help you chart out your goals and paths for the year. With this note, I wish you all a smooth journey ahead in whatever you do in 2018.

Warmest regards,

Dato' Joey Yap
July 2017

Connect with us:

www.joeyyap.com   www.joeyyap.tv

@DatoJoeyYap   @DJoeyYap   @JoeyYap

Academy website:
www.masteryacademy.com | jya.masteryacademy.com | www.baziprofiling.com

The Earthly Branches

In BaZi, the Earthly Branches on the BaZi Chart consist of the Four Pillars namely, the Hour, Day, Month and Year Pillars, as illustrated below. You need to refer to the forecast of each of the Animal Sign that appears on the respective Pillars of your BaZi Chart in order to derive a more comprehensive outlook for the year.

Each Pillar signifies a different aspect in life:

Internal		External	
Your inner personality and behaviour that are hidden from and not openly revealed to others.		The personality and behaviour you exhibit outwardly and can be seen by others.	
Hour Pillar denotes a person's dreams, hopes and inspirations.	**Day Pillar** represents an individual's relationship with his or her spouse.	**Month Pillar** reveals one's career and business outlook.	**Year Pillar** shows a person's state of health and social circle (i.e. friends).

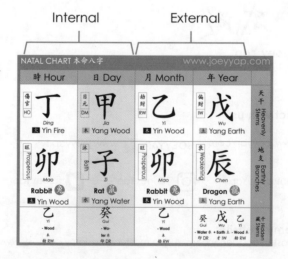

Do This First

Print your Free BaZi Chart at the URL below:

www.masteryacademy.com/regbook

Here is your unique code to access the BaZi Calculator:

CA12BZ68

Sample: This is how your BaZi Chart will look like

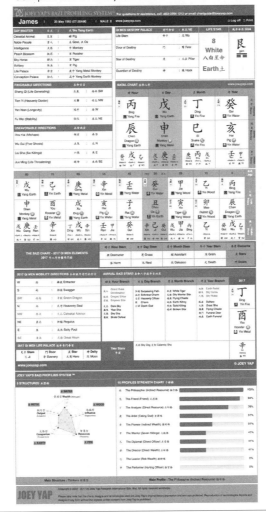

BONUS CONTENT

FREE DOWNLOAD

Exclusive content available for download with your purchase of the Chinese Astrology for 2018 book.

Claim your FREE ONLINE ACCESS now at:
www.masteryacademy.com/bookbonus2018

CAR81AC6 *Expires 31st December 2018*

Forecast for the 12 Animal Signs in 2018

Dog 戍

Year of the Dog							
1922	1934	1946	1958	1970	1982	1994	2006

A person's Chinese age is obtained by adding one year to their Western birthday. For example, if you were born in 1976, your Western age in 2018 is 42, but your Chinese age would be 43.

Overall Forecast For The Year

戌 2018 will likely be a mixed bag for you as you may find yourself faced with your fair share of personal and professional problems even as you attain the success you desire. Additionally, there is a chance that matters from one aspect of your life could spill over into others and be the underlying cause for the issues that arise in them. Despite all this, you will be able to overcome them as long as you remain optimistic and confident in yourself.

Where your career is concerned, you will have next to nothing to worry about due to the presence of the Elegant Seal Star (華蓋). Considered to be a truly auspicious star, it is ideal for those of you who have been seeking to advance their careers. There will be plenty of opportunities to prove yourself to your superiors and earn that promotion or raise that you so richly deserve. In fact, your confidence, sense of independence and overall luck in this aspect of your life are good reasons why you should consider pursuing any other professional interests you might have as well during this period.

Unfortunately, the boost to your work life may be one of the reasons why you could encounter problems in your personal one as the months go by. The Grand Duke (太歲) influence could trigger disruptions in your personal life as well as any plans you have made or are making at this point in time. It will be up to you to summon the same inner strength that you get in your job and rely on your own efforts to overcome the obstacles that you encounter. Whether you are able to do so or not will determine how successful you are at coming out on top.

There is also the chance of you running into financial problems to some extent more than once throughout the course of the year which could also cause its fair share of headaches. In order to mitigate and perhaps even solve this issue, you should do your best to budget yourself and spend your money wisely. It would also be for the best if you exercise caution when signing contracts and avoid financially risky activities such as gambling altogether.

Coupled with the appearance of the Hidden Corpse Star (伏屍) which carries with it the implication that things at home may not go smoothly, you should prepare yourself for some conflict in regard to your relationships. You may find yourself butting heads with your loved ones over a wide range of issues with one of them potentially being your career. In these trying times, it would be wise of you to always keep in mind that these people care about you. Come hell or high water, they are the ones who will be there for you and the disagreements you may be having at this point in time will never change that.

On the romance front, married couples and those in committed relationships will have to put in extra effort to make sure that minor disagreements among other things do not tear them apart. Being considerate, tolerant and willing to listen to each other will ensure that their bond remains strong. Meanwhile, those who are single might unfortunately not have much luck in finding love.

All this could also tie into the effects the Sword Edge Star (劍鋒) which could manifest in the form of health issues for you, this year. There is the possibility that a combination of your new work responsibilities and the turmoil in your personal life could negatively impact your well-being. You will be particularly vulnerable to suffering from a significant amount of stress and possibly even depression.

Nevertheless, this does not mean that 2018 will be more of a bad year than a good one. The key to ensuring that every aspect of your life and not just your career is in good shape is your own hard work and effort. Tackling whatever obstacles that pop up and settling any disagreements you have with others are things that are not easily accomplished but will be immensely rewarding if successfully done. In short, whether you can manage to have a good personal life as well as a professional one is entirely up to you.

The Forecast for Individual Aspects of the Year

 Wealth

In 2018, you might be constantly worried about a potential financial loss in your life. Thus, it is vital for you to spend your hard earned cash sensibly by effectively managing your personal finances. If these proper steps are not taken, you might discover that more money will be flowing out from your pocket than into it. Additionally, observe caution when signing new contracts as this too is an avenue that could lead to more financial loss. A weaker Indirect Wealth luck this year means that good fortune is not in your favour. Therefore, hitting the slot machines or heavy investing would be strongly ill-advised at this time and you should instead focus more on building up you savings.

 **Career**

Your work life is going to heavily drain you in several aspects. From being piled with a mountain of work-related pressure to dealing with your tough and ungrateful superiors, 2018 is going to be laced with conflicts that may lead to not only an unpleasant work space but also a worrying dip in your work productivity. Thus, consistency and determination is key to dealing with a tough year ahead at work. In addition to that, it is also unwise to move to another job position, which means you would have to contend with where you are for now and make the best out of the situation that you are currently in.

Relationships

Weak love prospects are in store for Dog individuals this year, which signals a trying time for couples to appropriately foster their relationship with each other. It is recommended that married couples practice an increase in tolerance and consideration in their relationship as even a simple misunderstanding could result in a significant decline in their bond. Single Dog individuals will be out of luck in terms of relationships prospects and they will probably have to lead a mostly isolated social life this year. If you are single, it is best to place your focus in improving other aspects of your life such as your health and work.

Health

This year's forecast for Dog individuals largely carries over from last year, as road safety is crucial to a healthier life. From the busy sidewalks to your on-road vehicles, accidents may happen at anytime and anyplace if you are not alert and it could lead to severe health injuries. Another physical health obstacle to be wary of is the use of metal items that could contain rust and other harmful materials on it. Therefore, refrain from constantly using metallic items to avoid any ill-health. Physiologically, you might experience certain digestive complications that would require you to diet and exercise more.

 **Monthly Luck**

農曆正月 (February 4th - March 4th) 甲寅

Overall, this month will bring good fortune into your life. Although there may be numerous inauspicious stars lurking about, however your luck will stay fairly consistent throughout. Plus, there are signs pointing to a surge of wealth on your horizon as well!

農曆二月 (March 5th - April 4th) 乙卯

Beware in this month, as there are certain obstacles at play here that could negatively halt your personal progress if it is not attended to. So long as you remain continuously motivated on the potential solutions, these obstacles will eventually clear away from your life path.

農曆三月 (April 5th - May 4th) 丙辰

A minor financial loss might be in your midst this month. However, there is no need for you to hit the panic button right away as this monetary loss will not leave a significant hole in your savings. You can still enjoy the fruits of our labour by purchasing things that you fancy to keep your mind off this matter.

農曆四月 (May 5th - June 5th) 丁巳

Luck shines upon those who are either looking for or are already in a relationship. So if you're single, throw yourself out there, mingle with others and you just might find that special someone for you! On the other hand, those in a committed relationship should carefully avoid those very things as your partner may misinterpret your intentions and it could lead both of you down a path of multiple heated arguments.

農曆五月 (June 6th - July 6th) 戊午

This month will be smooth sailing for you, as you will be granted the time and space to accomplish what you need to do, career-wise. You will even get a plethora of opportunities to display your talents front and centre for the world to see, so remember to tackle these moments with passion!

農曆六月 (July 7th - August 6th) 己未

Receive and celebrate the prosperity that the auspicious stars have gifted you this month. These prosperous gifts include getting to spend more quality time with your friends, which will bring the bonds of your friendships closer, and a positively steady outlook in your work life and wealth.

農曆七月 (August 7th - September 7th) 庚申

The good fortune granted upon you from last month will continue to spill into this month as well in almost every aspect of your life. One aspect that will not fare too well however is your work life, as you will encounter demanding work commitments that may weight you down emotionally. You're advised to manage your work wisely to evade an overload of work-related stress.

農曆八月 (September 8th - October 7th) 辛酉

Your health is of utmost importance as it enables you to strive for the goals you have set out for the year, and this month will bring some dangers to that precious health in terms of food poisoning. Show extreme caution regarding food cleanliness in what, where and how you eat so that your health will be preserved.

農曆九月 (October 8th - November 6th) 壬戌

The inauspicious trend continues here from last month, this time presenting a new danger altogether: extreme activities. From flesh wounds to fatal injuries, you should dodge any chances of putting yourself into high risk activities so that you come out unscathed from this perilous month.

農曆十月 (November 7th - December 6th) 癸亥

Wealth will be a "win some, lose some" scenario this month. As unpredictable as it is, but do not despair, as aid will swiftly arrive to your doorstep in the form of some kind and generous friends from your work. Therefore, continue to work diligently and professionally and these financial concerns will soon pass.

農曆十一月 (December 7th 2018 - January 4th 2019) 甲子

Your mind is filled with grand plans and ideas, and this month is the opportune time to put those mental gears into full throttle. You should make significant steps in creating and developing new projects at work and planning your future career path. Students would be wise to pour all their hard work and dedication into their studies to greatly improve their academic performance.

農曆十二月 (January 5th - February 3rd 2019) 乙丑

You will face obstacles around you that will try to hamper your development, especially at work. Thus, you work growth may be stunted this month as you will find it difficult to meet your work targets or please your superiors. Nevertheless, continue to push through it with determination and positivity and you will successfully resolve those obstacles.

Pig 亥

Year of the Pig							
1923	1935	1947	1959	1971	1983	1995	2007

A person's Chinese age is obtained by adding one year to their Western birthday. For example, if you were born in 1976, your Western age in 2018 is 42, but your Chinese age would be 43.

Overall Forecast For The Year

 The sky's the limit for you this coming year – blessed with the most positive Sun Star (太陽) and Sky Happiness Star (天喜), you could almost win and gain in any situation. The only person that may be holding you back is yourself. With a clear mind and by keeping yourself focused, you could achieve anything you set out to pursue in this Year of Dog!

Opportunities to gain and accumulate wealth as well as to open new doors in career and business would be plenty for you with the auspicious presence of the Sun Star. It will be a great year for you to showcase your capabilities and earn the career advancement or business development you have been eyeing for, as this is a positive period of time when the right people would be more willing to listen to you at the right time and the right place.

You will also need to be prepared for a heightened popularity with just about anyone this coming year; making friends would be a breeze as you seem to be able to say just the right words to brighten up any situation. People love having you in parties, gatherings, and also business meetings – you will have the chance to be influential. If you are an avid Instagrammer you will easily gain hundreds and thousands of likes; if you are making a business proposal, that would most possibly translate into investments you will be thrilled about.

It may be hard to keep a low profile in the coming year with both the Sun and the Sky Happiness Star present. The Sky Happiness Star favours knowledge and new relationships, giving those of you in the education industry or academia the productive fuel or creative juice you need to excel. This is also a very good sign for those of you who are graduating or getting married. No matter it is a graduation or a marriage, the Sky Happiness Star will definitely give you reasons to celebrate this coming year. For those who are single, this is also a positive year to look for a new love who is more likely to be a good match.

2018 has so much joy in store for you, if only you are willing to allow yourself to embrace opportunities and celebrate success. The presences of two stars indicating loneliness and isolation – the Solitary (孤辰) and the Sky Emptiness (天空) Stars – denote the danger of becoming entrapped in your own negativity. There are so many great things come knocking at your doorstep, yet you could feel insecure and unworthy of the good fortune.

You are the life of the party this coming year, but the hustle-bustle could also drain your liveliness and vigor. You may feel the need to withdraw and detach, and prolonged emotional state of feeling demoralised could cost you opportunities for wealth and relationship, if you choose to dwell in the negative emotions. Set out time for yourself away from work and people every week, to reflect and recharge despite your packed schedule; let yourself unwind and relax so that you could clear your mind and start anew without allowing negativity to burn you out.

Some me-time is essential for you to keep a healthy balance between business and pleasure. The presence of the Robbery Sha Star (劫煞) this coming year means you could also be easily persuaded and hence stray away from the path you should be taking. As you are blessed with all the right people willing to open their ears to you, you are also surrounded by people who want to thrust their opinions down your throats. If you are not careful with whose advice you trust, you could be taking unnecessary long winding paths before reaching your goals. Keep true to yourself and make sure you are surrounded by positive people so they can encourage and give you the nudge you need towards the right path.

All in all, 2018 is a year worth celebrating if you could keep yourself grounded and be open to seize new opportunities. The promise of wealth, career progression and new relationships are within your reach this coming year at just a sound decision away. Do not let your inner demons hold you back, or let the opinions of others lead you astray, and you are on the right track to reach the stars!

The Forecast for Individual Aspects of the Year

 **Wealth**

Early on in the year, you could undergo a barrage of obstacles that will prevent you from attaining extra financial wealth, whether it is stagnation in your business revenues or savings account. Do not fret however, as careful preparation and a positive demeanour will ensure a rapid resolution to these problems. From then on, you can anticipate a surge in your wealth as you might receive a well-deserved promotion or salary bonus. Money owed to you by your friends should be reimbursed back to you as soon as possible as there is a real possibility that people's pettiness could stall your money from being returned to you.

 **Career**

Minor obstacles that might disrupt your life in 2018 will be swiftly conquered over with some generous aid coming from your colleagues. These strong alliances will enable you to trounce over any resistance that could serve to undermine your work productivity and subsequently expand your windows of opportunity to showcase your hard work and talents to your superiors who will be highly appreciative of them.

Relationships

Celebrate the presence of the Sky Happiness Star (天喜) as your love will come furiously knocking on your door this year as opposed to the last year's dull forecast. 2018 will pepper your life with joyous events that will serve to further strengthen your relationship prospects. Long-term committed couples should capitalise on this ideal time to start concocting plans to get married before the year ends. Single Pigs can also rejoice on the notion that they might finally be able to start a romantic relationship if they stay vigilant in their social circles and confess their true feelings to that special someone.

Health

Your health prospects could take an unfortunate dive this year. Dangers to your health could appear in the form of physical injuries to physiological issues and they could stem from unknowingly participating in ill-fated events. However, the Sky Happiness Star can effectively shield you from these harmful omens as long as you practice a strict exercise regime and turn down any chance to perform extreme activities.

Monthly Luck

農曆正月 (February 4th - March 4th) 甲寅

A fairly auspicious month marks the start of your year, although you might get involved in a few commotions with your peers and colleagues. The reason for these ruckuses happening are insignificant, so keep your mind and body squarely focused on the goals you have set for yourself and remain morally principled throughout the entire scenario to ultimately enjoy a satisfactory work experience.

農曆二月 (March 5th - April 4th) 乙卯

Work life will be a smooth sailing experience where you will be significantly reducing your workload on your desk and your superiors will be delighted with the work performance you have been displaying. However, not every facet of your life will be rosy, especially in the health department. Ensure you get a sufficient dose of vitamins and minerals into your system and try not to exert yourself too much in certain activities.

農曆三月 (April 5th - May 4th) 丙辰

This month will herald a slight monetary loss from your pockets. Try not to dwell deeply on this unfortunate turn of events as it will not significantly affect your overall inflow of wealth. If you want, you can mitigate the situation by shopping at your favourite retail outlet to free your mind from the current financial distractions.

農曆四月 (May 5th - June 5th) 丁巳

Prime yourself adequately for a month filled with hectic scheduling, tight deadlines and superiors breathing down your neck. Use this experience to learn from your mistakes and you may still find a rosy outlook among all these thorny hurdles. Persist in churning out quality work output and eventually you might be greeted with a surprising salary increment or bonus.

豬

農曆五月 (June 6th - July 6th) 戊午

Your luck reverses its fortune in your favour this month as you will find helping hands from all corners of your life coming to lift you up from last month's hindrances and this month's annoyances. Therefore, your job outlook will be stable to allow a more productive work period. While you are at it, it is recommended that you cancel or postpone any high risk activities as the chances of physical injury are astonishingly prevalent.

農曆六月 (July 7th - August 6th) 己未

Bright stars of auspiciousness illuminate your night sky this month, granting you a well-deserved era of prosperity and stability in many aspects of your life. Take this opportunity to formulate some new plans in your personal and professional life that you would like to see come into fruition this month and it will pay dividends in the long run.

農曆七月 (August 7th - September 7th) 庚申

Fluctuating omens of auspiciousness and inauspiciousness could spell a volatile period for you this month. Thus, unlucky sequences of events might become more of norm for you than lucky ones. Remedying the current situation will take the utmost amounts caution and concentration from you. Take the longer but safer road in resolving these conflicts and ethically follow the standard regulations in existence.

農曆八月 (September 8th - October 7th) 辛酉

A month of uneasiness could plague your career this month. You might start to tremble in the wake of extra work targets and a fresh batch of work assignments on your desk which might lead you to constantly be trapped in a stressed out mind-set. Just like in the previous month, proceed with copious amounts of awareness and diligence and soon you will start to hit all those deadlines and cross off your workload by the time end of the month rolls around.

農曆九月 (October 8th - November 6th) 壬戌

Beware of the disruptions that will encapsulate this month as the tension in the air among your interactions in your social group could cause a set-back in your work progress. It is imperative that you mind your tone of your speech and always be civil in your encounters with others. In addition, avoid being a smart aleck and be open-minded to other perspectives.

農曆十月 (November 7th - December 6th) 癸亥

Although your unlucky streak continues into this month with new challenges standing in your way of growth, fortunately the presence the Relief God Star (解神) will reenergise your motivation to overcome any unforeseen obstructions that stand in your path and this month will end on a positive note for you.

農曆十一月 (December 7th 2018 - January 4th 2019) 甲子

The turbulent miscommunications that you experienced two months ago resurfaces to the forefront of your issues. Similar to a couple a months ago as well, proceed with patience when dealing with other people and carefully consider the phrasing of your message before you utter out in the open. You might also incur a slight loss of money during this time so try managing your finances appropriately. Other than that, tolerance and kindness will be vital to a harmonious family life should you want to pursue that.

農曆十二月 (January 5th - February 3rd 2019) 乙丑

This month, you would be wise to continue maintaining the polite and broad-minded approach that you adopted from last month when communicating with certain individuals in order to evade any hostile clashes later on. Try your best to not separate yourself from your monetary wealth by avoiding any dodgy investments schemes that appear in your line of sight.

Rat 子

Year of the Rat							
1924	1936	1948	1960	1972	1984	1996	2008

A person's Chinese age is obtained by adding one year to their Western birthday. For example, if you were born in 1976, your Western age in 2018 is 42, but your Chinese age would be 43.

Overall Forecast For The Year

2018 is the year for Rat individuals to take their personal development to the next level, thanks to appearance and support of the auspicious Eight Seats Star (八座). With its presence, expect a boost in your fortunes, in addition to enhanced ability to learn. Make the most of what this star brings by indulging in picking up new skillsets and improving on the ones you already have – perhaps by enrolling in some courses which may add value to your abilities. Those who are academicians, scholars or students will especially benefit from this powerful boost.

You may also find opportunities arising in the most unexpected way in terms of advancement, be it on a personal level or career-wise. It will benefit you greatly to keep an open mind and consider the many options life will place before you. All you need to do is to be observant enough to identify them. As such, be more sociable and meet new people as you will never know what pleasant surprises the next person you meet may bring. At the same time, keep those around you close as you will have a great affinity for finding the right people to support your endeavours. Don't be afraid to ask for advice or assistance whenever it is needed as your luck with Noble people is strong this year.

Rat individuals however will need to be extra careful this year due to the presence of several inauspicious stars associated with the heightened risk of accidents and injuries. The Blood Knife Star (血刃) is particularly known to increase the possibility of such occurrences, especially during physical activities. The Fu Chen Star (浮沉) implies that these accidents and injuries will be likely water-related, while the Flying Chaste Star (飛廉) indicates that much of these undesirable incidents will be due to one's carelessness or lack of attention. Due to this, it would be in the best interest of your own personal safety to be constantly vigilant not only around bodies of water, but at all times and anything you do to reduce the possibility of such outcomes.

With that said, there is no reason you should not enjoy water sports or leisure activities by the sea. You only need to be more cautious and make sure there is almost zero chance of accidents happening. For example, any plans to visit an island in the coming year for snorkelling and scuba diving should be taken with extra precautions. Ensure all safety measurements are in-check, and examine your equipment for any faultiness. You should also be more careful when you go for a swim. Try to swim in pools or beachside with a lifeguard nearby. It's also always good to swim with one or two friends, so when something unexpected happens, you have someone to get you help.

In the upcoming year, you may also need to pay more attention to the elderly members in your family, particularly those who are frail or may be suffering from deteriorating health, due to the presence of the Funeral Door (喪門) and the Earth Funeral (地喪) Stars. The two stars indicate possibility of illness and injuries harming an elderly family member or relative. However, do not be alarmed by what the names of the stars denote; the two stars do not necessary signify anyone passing away, but there may be a danger of someone taking a fall or a turn for the worse, so pay close attention to the elderly members and take them to the doctors when there are signs of declining health. They would need more support especially from you in 2018.

While it may seem worrying with the large presence of negative stars working against you this year, don't fret. The Relief God Star (解神) also happens to be visiting you this year which means much of the difficulties you will or might encounter would be diminished. The new year will bring you plenty of opportunities to excel and succeed, and you will be blessed with the ability to turn a negative situation into a positive one smoothly. While you may feel invincible riding a wave of success, you also have to be careful in regards to your own and elderly family members' well-being. Take all safety precautions, make sure you don't overstretch yourself, and always be on the lookout for your elderly family members; You will mostly likely gain more than lose this coming year!

The Forecast for Individual Aspects of the Year

 Wealth

Those born in the year of the Rat should brace themselves for a potential monetary loss due to unlucky financial investments or delayed reimbursements from money-borrowing friends. You can effectively counter this bad luck by wisely purchasing some real estate at the beginning of the year. Refrain from pouring your savings into any heavy investment schemes to avoid a huge financial loss, although some money might still flow out from your wealth vault. Overall, a smooth sailing financial year is in sight for you.

 **Career**

Prepare appropriately for a rocky year in your career life. Detach yourself from petty people and their nonsensical hindrances and focus squarely on advancing your career to new heights. Eventually the noises of these petty people will be gone and you will begin to reap the benefits of a promotion or a pay raise down the line. In addition, embrace the helping hands from the generous people in your life and your career in 2018 will be stable throughout.

 **Relationships**

2018 is a fairly strong year for those looking to start a romantic relationship. Thus, single Rats should keep an eye out in their social gatherings for that one person that could change your life for the better. Couples do not fare too well in the health sector this year as there is high chance that your significant other could be hospitalised for a serious affliction. Take up the fitness mantle in your relationship and encourage your partner to engage in a sport like jogging and compound both of your earnings to afford a healthier diet.

 **Health**

The Blood Knife Star (血刃) will appear in your midst this year so you might want to pay extra attention to your overall well-being. It would be wise for you to forgo any participation in extreme sports like hiking or heavy weightlifting to prevent any serious injury from transpiring. Despite this, do not despair for the manifestation of the Nobleman Star (貴人) will ensure that aid for your health predicaments is always close by.

 Monthly Luck

農曆正月 (February 4th - March 4th) 甲寅

Anticipate a fairly auspicious month to start off your lunar year. Your career will flow smoothly without much disruption and your family life will be relatively stable. Try to maintain this period of good luck as best as you can by mixing old-fashioned hard work and determination with fresh innovative ideas to tackle your responsibilities.

農曆二月 (March 5th - April 4th) 乙卯

Be careful with your words and actions as the chances of ending up in a heated row with your colleagues are quite high. As such, remember to remain humble in your interactions and restrain your ego from saying or doing something that you might regret later on. While you are at it, observe your environment to potentially receive a colossally joyous occasion.

農曆三月 (April 5th - May 4th) 丙辰

You will be swamped with unpredictability this month and so you must tread with caution if you want to see through the month in an optimistic manner. It is advisable that you abstain from developing any new projects or purchasing new assets and remain focus on what you are currently undertaking instead. The fickleness of this month might also cause some financial misery so sort your budget out beforehand.

農曆四月 (May 5th - June 5th) 丁巳

The volatile nature of last month's luck has finally stabilised this month although you might encounter a few stumbling blocks in your work and personal life. Adopt the strategy you used previously and continue to stay down-to-earth and industrious on your existing projects and success will be waiting for you around the corner.

農曆五月 (June 6th - July 6th) 戊午

The stars of auspiciousness and inauspiciousness collide this month which will see you coming across a mixed bag of positive and negative outcomes. In times like this, it is best to lay low and prepare a strong contingency plan to counter a possible deterioration in your wealth and health. Luck shines brightly over single people as they might hear wedding bells ringing in their near future should they initiate a relationship by professing their true feelings to the one they admire.

農曆六月 (July 7th - August 6th) 己未

Just like last month, this month's luck forecast bears an unstable mark as the Dark Sky (天厄) and Heavenly Sha (天煞) Stars cross paths. Unfortunately, you could be in attendance of someone's funeral service so exercise vigilance over the safety of your loved ones. Also, assume a level-headed attitude as you might also get disappointed with either someone else's or your determination in failing to push forward with your agenda. In the meantime, distance yourself from high risk activities that might cause serious physical injury to you.

農曆七月 (August 7th - September 7th) 庚申

This month's auspiciousness should be able to quell the misfortunes that might pop up on your radar. However, do not depend solely on the arrival of this good luck as you might run into some bumps with your finances and health if these lucky stars do not pan out consistently. It is crucial that you closely watch over your finances from the likelihood of loss or theft and maintain a dietary routine to remain clean from any illnesses.

農曆八月 (September 8th - October 7th) 辛酉

Caution yourself when you are making deals in situations that will likely have an extensive impact in the months to come. From making personal decisions to brokering huge business transactions, always take a step back and look at the broader picture twice before you jump into a decision making stage or else you might see those verdicts backfire.

農曆九月 (October 8th - November 6th) 壬戌

This is the month where you can get these creative juice flowing. Start to execute ideas and new schemes that you have in your head and putting them into action. Moreover, the dynamic duo, which is the Nobleman (貴人) and Sky Relief (天解) Stars, combined with your tenacity and resourcefulness will guide you out of any obstacles in your path.

農曆十月 (November 7th - December 6th) 癸亥

To design a financial budget that would limit you spend lavishly. Those looking to expand their wealth accumulation should take this opportunity start expanding their investment portfolio or develop new career advancement plans to elevate their income and status.

農曆十一月 (December 7th 2018 - January 4th 2019) 甲子

It is highly recommended that you abstain from acting recklessly when you are on the verge of closing a huge contract or when you are deciding on certain familial issues because you might only exacerbate the situation into negativity. Rationalise every single decision that you might come upon step by step and you should see through the month without a hitch.

農曆十二月 (January 5th - February 3rd 2019) 乙丑

The end of the lunar year spells an unbalanced projection of auspiciousness for you. Certain things might work out in your favour as you work to accomplish all the necessary workload on your plate with uninterrupted efficiency. In terms of inauspiciousness, it should only affect you in the form of financial loss and arguments that could escalate to a legal battle. Have faith in your ability to overcome these obstructions and you will prosper in this period.

Year of the Ox							
1925	1937	1949	1961	1973	1985	1997	2009

A person's Chinese age is obtained by adding one year to their Western birthday. For example, if you were born in 1976, your Western age in 2018 is 42, but your Chinese age would be 43.

Overall Forecast For The Year

丑 This upcoming year sees strong potentials in terms of wealth accumulation and career advancement for you. With the presence of two very auspicious stars, not only are you able to have the Midas touch, you would also receive assistance from Noble people when you need it. With such bountiful rewards bestowed to you, practicing the middle way of moderation and keeping a healthy balance are the keys to truly enjoy the gifts of the universe.

If you are looking to invest or advance in your career, the year 2018 will send good news your way with the presence of the Moon Star (太陰), an auspicious sign of wealth and prosperity. Your ability to increase your wealth will be greatly enhanced; whether it's a promotion at your work, or a positive return from an investment, you are bound to see some improvements. This will be a good year for you to improve and strengthen your financial standing so explore the opportunities whenever possible. For those of you seeking to accrue wealth in preparation for a marriage or a family, this is your golden opportunity.

The Yin nature of the Moon Star indicates female-dominated industries would be more likely to prosper this coming year; timely assistance would also be more likely to come from women in life. Together with the presence of the Heavenly Yi Star (天乙), you will benefit greatly from the help of women in 2018. They are willing to give you a hand when you ask for it; some of them may also offer secret assistance when you least expect it. If you are proposing a plan, they could be the ones giving your plan the push needed for green light, with or without you knowing it. If you are facing challenges at work, a female senior manager would be likely to offer you helpful advice or even be the one recommending you for a promotion.

Besides being in the good books of the women in your life would benefit you hugely, it is also a favourable time for you to start or run a business in female-dominated industries such as fashion and beauty. With support from the National Treasure Star (國印), you will find that your efforts will bear fruit easily. As long as you strive to hit all the right targets, the rewards are almost certainly guaranteed.

Your good luck however could be tainted if you indulge in the excess of wealth and opportunities without keeping your ego in check. Four stars related to miscommunications are present in the Year of Dog, and if you let yourself get carried away by triumphs and money, you may risk hurting the feelings of those surrounding you with careless words. The presences of the Piercing Rope (貫索) and the Annual Sha (年煞) Stars indicate possible gossip and bad blood with the people around you; their negative influences strengthened by the presence of the Broken Star (破碎), which may put your reputation at stake if you are not cautious. Confusion and uncertainty will arise when it seems like every word you say gets interpreted in a way you do not intend to, as there is also the presence of the Hook Spirit Star (勾神). Keep level-headed and practice self-restrain at all times, in bad times and even more so in good times, and you could wade through this fog of words unharmed with new enlightenment.

Staying calm and sensible is important also because of the presences of the Solid Killing (的煞) and the Great Assembly (卒暴) Stars that increase the risk of losing valuable items and getting injured. Be extra careful and attentive to your personal items, jewelry, and documents; double-check every time you get down from a taxi for your belongings, and remember to backup any important documents. While you enjoy the extravagances the coming year brings, you should also pay extra care to your health. Practice moderation in everything you do and most importantly, do not drink and drive. Safety should be your priority.

This new year, the world is your oyster; you only need to be cautious and considerate in your words and actions to fully enjoy the prosperous year. In turn, you could share your good luck with those surrounding you. While plenty wealth opportunities await in the Year of Dog, don't forget to take good care of your health and belongings. Remember it's always better to be safe than sorry. Now, get ready for a wonderful new year and welcome your good fortune with open arms!

The Forecast for Individual Aspects of the Year

 **Wealth**

In 2018, the Moon Star (太陰) of your Year Palace illuminates over you as it foretells a wonderful year of wealth accumulation. You could very likely witness a surprising pay rise at your job through bonuses or a promotion. However, take careful notice of your finances, you are advised to wisely invest in some decent real estate and strictly avoid any chance to part with your wealth through risky financial investment.

 Career

A smooth sailing situation is on the horizon for your career this year as there will be little to no fluctuations in regards to your work. The inauspicious Broken Star (破碎) could still cause some significant disruptions in your work environment between you and your colleagues. Carry on in stride however, as it is said that those who are not envied are mediocre. Thus, compose yourself around your peers at work and continue display diligence and your colleagues will eventually come to respect you and provide you some aid when necessary.

 **Relationships**

2018 will prove to be a less than stellar year for those who are single due to the absence of the Peach Blossom Luck in your Palace. Instead of feeling hopeless in their romantic prospects, single Ox individuals should still socialise and mingle with the opposite sex as they might still have a chance of discovering their one true love. Those who are already in a loving and stable relationship should consider moving forward with their wedding plans.

 **Health**

This year marks the presence of an inauspicious star in your Palace, implying a negative turn of events relating to your well-being. Medical receipts might become a normal sight for you if you fail to take heed of your health. Should you contract a serious illness, it is highly recommended that you take a trip to the doctor's office to swiftly address and not allow it to fester. Observe a healthy diet and consider taking up a sport to maintain your physical fitness to mitigate these issues.

Monthly Luck

農曆正月 (February 4th - March 4th) 甲寅

This month could see your luck on a see-saw as some things may or may not work out as planned. Avoid making radical decisions that might be regrettable in the long run and steer yourself with calmness and caution. Make calculated steps in every facet of your life. Other than that, you will come across rather favourable fortunes in this period.

農曆二月 (March 5th - April 4th) 乙卯

Despite all the people around you, this month could see you become increasingly isolated due to a sudden lack of assistance and support from your co-workers. Independence and diligence will be vital to get you through an exhausting month, especially when your work performance goes unnoticed by your superiors and you have to go at it alone due to desertion from your work peers.

農曆三月 (April 5th - May 4th) 丙辰

Keep a close watch on your finances this month as substantial amounts money might slip away from you as denoted by the presence the Heavenly Sha. Under no circumstances should you affiliate yourself with any extreme activities that could bring risk of severe injuries. Lending money to people is also inadvisable as they might not have the means to pay you back in the future, so it will be in your best interest to turn away any request unless it is from someone that you can absolutely trust.

農曆四月 (May 5th - June 5th) 丁巳

Auspicious stars are aligned in your favour this month. Plans that you have cooked up from prior months will carry safely over to this month to ensure a smooth schedule free of any nuisance and disruptions. This relatively stress free period will put you in a good mood so long as you adopt a positive outlook in your future endeavours.

農曆五月 (June 6th - July 6th) 戊午

Temptations this month could possibly destroy your steady relationship with your significant other. Distance yourself from acting on potentially amorous feelings towards those outside of your relationships or else it could lead to an irreparable breakdown between you and your partner. Furthermore, you may find yourself enveloped by feelings of helplessness at work due to circumstances beyond your control. Persevere through these frustrations and maintain a stable effort in your endeavours. You should see through the month without major hassles.

農曆六月 (July 7th - August 6th) 己未

Things may not go smoothly this month with some obstacles appearing to disrupt your efforts to devise some concrete strategies to achieve your goals. As unpromising as this month might look from the surface, resolve to work hard in discovering solutions to these issues so that you can get back on track to meet the objectives you have devised for yourself.

農曆七月 (August 7th - September 7th) 庚申

Your luck appears to be modest this month and there might just be a few hiccups along the road. Keep your eyes peeled and heart open. There should be some favourable events occurring in your social circles. Signs also allude to a bountiful rewards in terms of money. Consider expanding your investment portfolio to welcome extra income into your life.

農曆八月 (September 8th - October 7th) 辛酉

Lucky stars shine bright over you as you head into a month absent of negativity and disturbances. You will receive due recognition for your efforts at your job and students can expect some positive scores when their examination results are released. Take the necessary course of action to capitalise on this good fortune and the returns will definitely be worthwhile.

農曆九月 (October 8th - November 6th) 壬戌

A dip in your luck from last month could see you falling out with multiple people you hold dear in your social life this month. Thus, colleagues and superiors at work might not come to your rescue should you land yourself in a sticky predicament at work. Try to be more forgiving of their behaviour, as they might not realise the effect of their actions on your situation. Moreover, stay humble by socialising with your work peers during and outside work to foster a strong bond with them in the long run.

農曆十月 (November 7th - December 6th) 癸亥

Be prepared for a hectic time this month, and you can expect increased pressure from family commitments, increased work assignments and busy academic revision periods. The energy drain might be severe as you try to meet all these objectives, but as the saying goes, "Rome wasn't built in a day". Thus, sufficient rest and persistence will be needed as you slowly but surely tick all the boxes of your to-do list.

農曆十一月 (December 7th 2018 - January 4th 2019) 甲子

After last month's lacklustre forecast, in comes a wealth of good fortune which will shine the way on all your prospects. There will be excellent possibilities to substantially grow your career and the financial gain will be enormous. It is advisable that you scout out new opportunities to invest your hard earned money and lay out a game plan on how you might want to take your career to the next level.

農曆十二月 (January 5th - February 3rd 2019) 乙丑

Obstructions in your way this month may prove to be a hindrance to all the effort you have been pouring into realising your ambitions. This situation could see misfortunes occurring when you least expect it. To alleviate the situation, consider utilising your finances wisely and perhaps look to performing some charitable deeds.

Tiger 寅

虎

The Tiger in 2018

Year of the Tiger								
1914	1926	1938	1950	1962	1974	1986	1998	2010

A person's Chinese age is obtained by adding one year to their Western birthday. For example, if you were born in 1976, your Western age in 2018 is 42, but your Chinese age would be 43.

Overall Forecast For The Year

This year might be a bumpy one for you as both welcome and unwelcome events play out over the course of the next 12 months of your life. Wealth and success in the business and professional aspects of your life can be expected although they may not be handed to you on a silver platter. Some effort on your part will be required but do not be afraid to put in the hard work as you will be richly rewarded. Unfortunately, there will be obstacles in both your personal and professional lives which will test your ability to stay on top of everything.

If you have been harbouring concerns about the trajectory and future of your career, you can rest assured as 2018 will be a good year for you. The positive energies of the Three Stages Star (三台) will provide a significant boost to your professional ambitions. If you are working in a company, expect opportunities to showcase your talents, earn yourself a raise or even climb the corporate ladder. On the off chance that you own a business, you can look forward to lucrative chances and deals which will allow you to increase your profit margins and also expand your business.

Nevertheless, none of these things will simply fall into your lap and positive outcomes are not a blanket guarantee if you do not do your part in making them a reality. The Earth Killing Star's (地煞) presence indicates that it will still be necessary for you to make solid plans and sound strategies in order to achieve your goals. This is especially true as there could be disruptions to your work or the projects you are involved in such as delays which can be easily addressed with well thought-out solutions. On the plus side, such incidents will only help to highlight the need for there to be a significant amount of attention to detail in order for things to get done quickly and properly.

There is also the possibility of some entirely unwanted fallout from your soaring career prospects and success in the form of jealousy and resentment from those around you due to the appropriately-named Back Poking Star (指背). These green-eyed monsters could try to bring you down by spreading malicious lies and rumours about you, leading to misunderstandings between you and the people who are important to you. You should also brace yourself mentally for excessively harsh criticisms directed at you from overly-competitive individuals. Additionally, you should be wary of who you choose to trust as they may turn around and betray your confidence somehow.

Meanwhile, another source of concern is the combined presence of the Flying Charm (飛符), Officer Charm (官符) and Year Charm (年符) Stars which all carry implications of legal entanglements. If this happens, there is a distinct possibility that it involves people who wish you harm due to your professional success. In order to avoid falling into their trap, you will have to handle all your interactions with others with great care and be careful to not make the kind of mistakes that will lead to this unwanted outcome.

Aside from legal troubles, it should be noted that the Year Charm Star also heralds the potential for unwanted chaos in your life, especially when it comes to money. This ties into the Swallow Trap Star's (吞陷) negative influence on your financial status. You are thus strongly advised to manage your finances well and be very cautious when making any significantly large transactions. That means it would be for the best if you avoid making any large investments or even lending money to others as you may not get it back.

It should be noted that having to deal with all this could cause you some measure of mental and emotional distress as indicated by the Five Ghost Star (五鬼). The strain of having to juggle a career that is flourishing by leaps and bounds with its less desirable side-effects may cause you some measure of anxiety. In such a situation, emotional volatility is completely understandable but letting it consume you will not do you any good at all. You have to control yourself and not give in to it as it will only make you act rashly and impatiently which in turn will have repercussions on every aspect of your life.

虎

The Forecast for Individual Aspects of the Year

 **Wealth**

This year could indicate some early financial losses on your side due to poor investment returns or mismanaged budgeting. However, your problems will be mitigated somewhat by the presence of a Noble Person. This Noble Person will ensure that you acquire the necessary assets that you desire, despite your constant spending throughout the year. Consider donating to a charitable organisation that you greatly admire as well as a way of paying it forward for the assistance you receive from others.

 Career

Some disputes resulting from misunderstandings with your superiors and colleagues could be expected this year. It would be in your best interest to be watchful of your interactions with others at work lest you unknowingly offend someone. Additionally, you should be vigilant of certain malicious colleagues looking to double-cross you. The presence of the Three Stages Star (三台) should assist you in alleviating some of this workplace hostility as long as you do your part in improving your communication competency at work. This will help you to avoid further office disputes from occurring in the future.

 **Relationships**

Since the Three Stages Star (三台) signifies a sense of togetherness, unmarried couples in a loving relationship should strongly contemplate the notion of marriage in their near future to solidify their bond. Although the Peach Blossom Luck is absent in 2018, single people looking to get into a worthwhile relationship should continue to search for a suitable person to propose their love to. This is because the Three Combinations Star shines upon single Tiger individuals as well.

 **Health**

Extra vigilance is advised during this year in regards to your health due to the manifestation of inauspicious stars in your Palace. Start a new trend of maintaining your hygiene and observing a healthier diet with all the necessary vitamins and minerals in tow. Your body's immune system will then be ready for any diseases that might attack your body. Invite people from your social circle who might want to join you in performing physical activity in a team sport. And as always, be wary of circumstances that could cause you to contract a certain illness and seek immediate medical treatment if you do fall sick.

 Monthly Luck

農曆正月 (February 4th - March 4th) 甲寅

Things may not go smoothly this month. Results produced at work might not be up to standard with your superiors' expectations and this could cause you to feel inefficient in your overall job productivity. Do not torture yourself over these perceived inadequacies and instead keep your mind squarely focused on creating your best work. Regardless of the kind of results your work might produce initially, eventually your superiors will start to view your work outcomes favourably.

農曆二月 (March 5th - April 4th) 乙卯

Luck with the opposite sex will be fruitful this month. Therefore, single Tiger individuals should keep their eyes open on potentially getting into a serious relationship with someone they adore. At your workplace, you may find more colleagues of the opposite sex coming to your aid a little more than usual. Keep in mind however that this support may not be fully beneficial to the larger issues that you might be facing. Instead, you should plan out your strategy for tackling these bigger matters independently.

農曆三月 (April 5th - May 4th) 丙辰

The Moon Sha Star (太陰) marks its presence this month. Hence, pay close attention to your familial connections. Your interaction with your family members would be more scarce than usual due to mounting work taking up your personal time. Try to schedule time as much as you can with your family members, from small lunch dates to watching television shows at home together. This will maintain the strength of your family ties during this trying month.

農曆四月 (May 5th - June 5th) 丁巳

Certain obstacles arrive this month to impede your work efficiency. Similar to last month's forecast, it is wise to brace yourself for longer hours of being stuck in the office trying to meet your deadlines. This could also negatively affect your household relationships as well. As isolated as you might feel at this time, you should remain patient and resilient, and see out this month in an optimistic manner.

農曆五月 (June 6th - July 6th) 戊午

After a couple of turbulent months, the Three Stages Star (三台) graces you with its influence this month. This auspicious star will bring you with a timely enhancement to your personal reputation in your social circles. Close friends and distant acquaintances will arrive to lend a helping hand to sort out any difficulties you might have at work or in your finances. This means that a promising outlook for your career and wealth will be in store for you.

農曆六月 (July 7th - August 6th) 己未

Exercise extra caution over your well-being this month to avoid being affected by any afflictions that could degrade your health. Whether physical hazards on the road or physiological issues in your body, it is imperative that you observe a healthy lifestyle during this period. Additionally, a Noble Person in the form of your physician or a close ally would be at your side to take care of your needs should you become ill or injured.

農曆七月 (August 7th - September 7th) 庚申

This month will bring some fluctuating luck. In the beginning, unfortunate occurrences might transpire in your family, finances, or career. This will potentially deter you from carrying out any conceived plans in those areas. Do not fret however, for the influence of the Earth Relief Star (地解) will soon steer through all these negativity when you approach each situation with care and forethought.

農曆八月 (September 8th - October 7th) 辛酉

Your auspicious prospects look great this month, with your career making good headway and your familial bonds becoming tighter than ever. In addition, you might finally be able to execute your long-gestating plans uninterrupted. Continue to be prudent about your well-being by eating healthy meals regularly and working out rigorously or else you might end up falling sick more often than usual.

農曆九月 (October 8th - November 6th) 壬戌

Just like last month, lucky stars continue to work for you this month. This might heavily imply an abundance of career advancement opportunities and opportunities to grow your wealth. Take advantage of this favourable time to impress your superiors and colleagues with your productivity and you might see a substantial pay raise in the near future. As noted by the presence of the White Tiger Star (白虎), petty people from your workplace will try to tarnish these favourable prospects. It is advisable that you stay vigilant and disciplined when communicating with your colleagues to avoid these issues from dampening your luck prospects.

農曆十月 (November 7th - December 6th) 癸亥

Your lucky streak continues into this month's forecast due to the presence of the Nobleman Star (貴人). You may see a lot of generous individuals, known or unknown, coming to your aid when you need it the most. Be sure to practice kind and open communication when accepting these compassionate gestures. If you do this, all your ideas and plans could be successfully implemented without a hitch.

農曆十一月 (December 7th 2018 - January 4th 2019) 甲子

Steady yourself this month as you will encounter various obstacles during this period. Remember that times like these call for tolerance and persistence on your part so that you can swiftly discover feasible solutions to these problems. Moreover, it is highly recommended that you commence working on grander projects next month. This is due to the presence of certain obstacles that might significantly hamper your projects' progress if it were to be executed this month.

農曆十二月 (January 5th - February 3rd 2019) 乙丑

The lunar year comes to a close with the presence of Peach Blossom Luck in your romantic life this month. Thus, this is the ideal time for single Tiger individuals to pursue the person whom they have always cherished and create a successful relationship out of that rich intimacy. On the other hand, take care of your health this month by dieting properly and becoming proactive in physical activities to effectively counter the harmful illnesses that the Sickness Charm Star (病符) brings.

Rabbit 卯

Year of the Rabbit								
1915	1927	1939	1951	1963	1975	1987	1999	2011

A person's Chinese age is obtained by adding one year to their Western birthday. For example, if you were born in 1976, your Western age in 2018 is 42, but your Chinese age would be 43.

Overall Forecast For The Year

卯 This new year, expect to be surrounded by abundance of love and support with two strongly auspicious stars present! The Grand Duke Combination Star (歲合) strengthened with the Monthly Virtue Star (月德) means 2018 will be a smooth sailing path for you, paired with the assistance of kind and generous people around you. While you are swept off your feet by a social whirlwind, don't forget to also give your family the attention they may need.

With the Grand Duke Combination and the Monthly Virtue Stars present in 2018, you may find it difficult to keep to yourself, there is no reason to stay aloof, for you will greatly benefit from the assistance of Noble people that would surround you this wonderful new year. If you are aiming for career growth, you will easily find experienced mentors that will share their knowledge generously, and guide you to your success at work; all you need to do is ask and assistance will come to you. Knowing and befriending the right people will get you far.

The combination of these two stars boosts the positive influence of new relationships. Get ready to be invited to gatherings and events where you will meet a lot of new people, and gain tremendous benefits from making new collaborations and partnerships which will most likely to be in your favour. New friends you make will be happy to lend you support and share their insights with you, giving you the extra edge and motivation in job hunting, business investments and career advancement. Don't be shy to add more Facebook friends or LinkedIn connections!

All the glitz and glamour you get to enjoy in 2018 may tempt you to overstretch yourself and lose track of your finances. The Lesser Consumer Star (小耗) suggests cash outflow that is more of a result of recklessness and extravagant spending, so it is advisable to keep a record of your spending this new year, and make sure you don't spend a lot more than you need to. With Noble support available in the coming year, you are also likely to get helpful advice on personal finance management. You could also get good recommendations for useful apps to manage your budget.

With so much happening for you in the Year of Dog, you may be left with little time to take care of your family and your loved ones, but they deserve your attention as much as your friends and work. The presences of the Death Charm (死符) and the Salty Pool (咸池) Stars are reminders not to take your family and your loved ones for granted. Pay extra attention to the senior members in your family, especially elderly gentlemen, as minor health risks may be present. They may not want to distract you from your ambitions and keep their mouths sealed about any sickness, so spending more time with your family can make it easier for you to spot if anything is amiss.

If you are married or in a committed relationship, be cautious of temptations and dalliances due to the presence of the Salty Pool Star. Betrayals not only hurt your partner, but also your reputation as scandals tend to spread fast. Likewise, it is almost impossible to keep your significant other in the dark if you have a fling, for he or she would catch wind of your secret affair sooner than later. Flings are most possibly not worth pursuing, and you will do well to spend more quality time with your spouse or significant other. Get back to the comfort of your home and family earlier when possible, and make plans for weekends to strengthen bonds.

2018 brings to you the right people and assistance you need to succeed. All you need to do is make sure you know the questions to ask and don't let yourself be carried away by the extravagances bestowed to you this brand new year. While you get the access to success, remember to take care of your family and loved ones, who are most likely also the ones giving you the most vital support in life. It will be a year filled with fun, laughter and good times, so sit back, relax, and get ready for this fabulous new year!

The Forecast for Individual Aspects of the Year

 **Wealth**

In 2018, be especially prudent about your finances as you could lose track of it if you are not vigilant. A variety of bad luck in the form of legal, personal or professional disputes could see you sustain a significant financial loss, so monitor both your money and also your social interactions with others. In terms of income, you can expect a plethora of opportunities from kind people to increase your overall wealth. Overall, this year is a profitable year to gain substantial financial wealth.

 Career

This year, your career will experience an abundance of auspicious tidings with the Grand Duke Combination Star (歲合). You will start to get along with your superiors and this blossoming rapport could lead to increased opportunities to showcase your abilities at work. However, you should always practice a precautionary and stable work ethic on your end or else you might overwork yourself to a risky fatigue level.

兔

 **Relationships**

As far as couples are concerned, quarrelsome behaviour might easily catalyse between you and your loved one with the level of disagreements ranging from trivial to weighty. Nonetheless, 2018 will bring about a lot of peace-making opportunities for both you and your partner to benefit from, in order to stabilise the relationship. Couples who are just beginning to sow the seeds of their bond should be tolerant and considerate of each other's persona or the relationship might meet an early demise.

 **Health**

Regarding your well-being, this year may signal a negative turn of events with more illnesses and injuries entering your life. However, this year also grants you the opportunity to boost your overall well-being. As long as you are dieting properly and exercising sufficiently, you can lessen your chances of contracting ailments considerably. Thereafter, you can enjoy an enriching lifestyle this year.

Monthly Luck

農曆正月 (February 4th - March 4th) 甲寅

Ideally, this would be the month for you to start packing your luggage and fly to your favourite vacation spot abroad. The alternative to taking a holiday looks much bleaker as you might be swarmed with a pile of workload that will keep you trudging at the office until midnight. So relax and take that long-gestating trip and come back to work later with a fresh resolve. Your travels could even impact your socialisation skills positively as you will likely encounter several conversational issues during this time.

農曆二月 (March 5th - April 4th) 乙卯

The appearance of the Punishments Stars (刑星) should alert you to observe vigilance throughout this unlucky month. Through no fault of your own, you might unintentionally offend malicious individuals who might plot your downfall in secret by spreading gossip about your words in order to turn others against you. Your communication with your family and friends could also land you in additional hot water. So be wary about what you might imply when you speak to people. Additionally, refrain from engaging in extreme activities that might easily harm you.

農曆三月 (April 5th - May 4th) 丙辰

A favourable change of fortune from last month's inauspicious forecast is on your way this month. A spirited and energetic drive will consume your work ethic with plenty of successful performances to show for it. Spin that creative mind of yours to contribute more in your job and you will stand to gain substantial appreciation from your superiors.

農曆四月 (May 5th - June 5th) 丁巳

Aid will arrive to you when you need if from kind-hearted people, due to the presence of the Nobleman Star (貴人) this month. Therefore, your work will run smoothly when you start to accept the generosity from your peers at work. Embrace the real estate and jewellery markets with your hard earned money because you will be able to acquire them with a more affordable price than before.

農曆五月 (June 6th - July 6th) 戊午

Downsize any mega plans you might be concocting or avoid any project that could breed significant consequences during this month as a volley of obstacles might be thrown at you if choose to participate in a large project. So, delay those giant ventures for now in order to reap the full rewards that these endeavours could bring in the future.

農曆六月 (July 7th - August 6th) 己未

Your luck will land on rocky terrain this month as you will discover that fortune might not always be on your side. Even the simplest of job assignments may prove to be an almighty hurdle for you to jump over, only barely meeting your deadlines. It is highly advisable that you organize your priorities in order and devote additional time to complete your workload after working hours to triumph over this difficult phase.

農曆七月 (August 7th - September 7th) 庚申

As opposed to last month, this month will greet you in an auspicious tone that will bump up your energy levels and positivity. Make use of this opportunity to spearhead some major development in your work tasks and personal plans and you will find that your efficiency will be duly remunerated by the time the end of this month rolls around.

農曆八月 (September 8th - October 7th) 辛酉

Single Rabbits should embrace the Peach Blossom Luck that is present this month as your romantic prospects will be given a huge boost. So persist in your socialisation with the opposite sex to find that special someone that grabs your heart and confess your love to them to possibly blossom a fruitful relationship. Couples already belonging in a loving relationship can further fortify their bond by participating in more activities together.

農曆九月 (October 8th - November 6th) 壬戌

This month will see a myriad of incoming obstacles to burden your personal and work life. You may find your superiors frustrated with your work output and you family might feel disappointed with the lack of time you spend with them. However, if you balance your time and effort effectively in both of the aforementioned aspects, the presence of the Six Combinations Star (六合) should aid you in resolving these matters in time.

農曆十月 (November 7th - December 6th) 癸亥

Last month's inauspicious trend will continue well into this month as obstacles continue to plague your life. You might even feel that the weight of these problems could overwhelm you at any moment as every decision you make backfires against you. Just like last month, continue to manage your priorities in an efficient manner and try to learn the lessons that this tough month is trying to teach you.

農曆十一月 (December 7th 2018 - January 4th 2019) 甲子

Meetings with your lawyer and court hearings might become a norm for you this month. Minor misunderstandings could turn ugly as some troublemakers will try to pull your spirits down with all these litigations. Caution yourself when speaking to other individuals to prevent your message from being misconstrued by conniving individuals.

農曆十二月 (January 5th - February 3rd 2019) 乙丑

Your lunar year ends on fairly positive note as this month will prove to be fairly auspicious for your endeavours. You might stumble upon a few barriers in the beginning but soon these hardships will dissipate as long as you are tenacious in finding the solutions. Therefore, freely engage in any plans or activities that pique your interest and spend more time with the ones who are close to you.

Dragon 辰

Year of the Dragon							
1928	1940	1952	1964	1976	1988	2000	2012

A person's Chinese age is obtained by adding one year to their Western birthday. For example, if you were born in 1976, your Western age in 2018 is 42, but your Chinese age would be 43.

Overall Forecast For The Year

辰 The new year will see turbulence and challenges in store for you, which you have the ability to turn them into opportunities for personal growth. With several stars indicating challenges present, changes and setbacks are most likely to be inevitable in 2018, but it is how you play your cards that could turn a bad hand into a favourable situation for you.

You may start this Year of Dog feeling motivated to set your plans in motion as soon as possible, but with the presence of the Leopard Tail (豹尾) and the Obstacle (闌干) Stars, you may have to take one step back every time you take two steps forward. The two stars indicate that you may need to work harder than usual to achieve your goals in the coming year, as a result of unforeseen circumstances. If you are planning to expand your business or take on large scale projects, make sure you consider all possible situations and have sufficient resources to cover all scenarios, so your plans will not fall through due to lack of money, manpower or communication. Be prepared for the worst and you will have nothing to worry about.

This upcoming year, you will also have the company of the Month Emptiness (月空) Star, which may encourage you to dream bigger, but these dreams are not necessarily realistic. You are no stranger to challenges and you are ready to surmount any obstacles on the path to your goals. However, you are advised to review your goals and ambitions before 2018. You may feel optimistic about handling new plans and projects, but you have to be careful of biting off more than you can chew. You will do well to carefully consider all possible turns of events, and honestly judge your own capabilities, before you pursue goals and dreams that may be lofty and unrealistic.

Trying to reach impractical goals will do you no good, as it will pose danger of allowing yourself to be unnecessarily demoralised, stressed and anxious. Instead of shooting for the moon this coming year, you would do better working on what is right in front of you. Consider taking your foot off the pedal, slow down to embrace the present, sharpen your skills and be prepared for 2018. It may turn out to be beneficial for you. Let challenges encourage you to grow, but do not let minor setbacks in life drag you down.

Strengthened by the influence of the Month Emptiness (月空) and the Great Consumer (大耗) Stars present in 2018 could also mean the tendency to spend money aimlessly. You may be tempted to gamble on huge investments or be careless on grand expenditure in terms of home and lifestyle. You may want to splurge on buying luxurious condominiums, signing up expensive gym memberships and enrolling in long-term courses and classes. These investments may benefit you, but you may want to think twice of what exactly you are trying to get out of these splurges. On the contrary, a feasible saving plan may put you in a more advantageous position in light of the challenges and changes in 2018.

Changes can bring positive or negative outcomes, and you will find unexpected changes that are often hard to negotiate in the upcoming year with the presence of the Year Breaker (歲破). The star denotes unsettling changes to long-standing situations, so you may have to be prepared for losing the upper hand you always had. However, as changes also bring opportunities, you can make changes work in your favour by accepting and making the most out of them instead of trying to go against the tides. The presence of the Monthly Sha Star (月煞) also indicates problems regarding women in your life, but you can easily resolve these issues with honest communication and by remaining calm.

If you have always been busy making plans and making them work in the past few years, you now have the chance to slow down and learn to live in the moment in 2018. Embrace changes with an open mind, enjoy the little things in every moment, and you will find yourself feeling more alive than ever. When the coming year ends, the obstacles that do not break you will make you even stronger and you will be able to accomplish more in the future.

The Forecast for Individual Aspects of the Year

 **Wealth**

This year, you might experience a constant monetary loss. In order to face to this challenge, you should formulate a suitable financial plan and budget in order to successfully manage your financial outlook. Inadequate financial planning and a lack of caution in making financial deals in 2018 could potentially lead to an outflow of money. 2018 is the year of a weak Indirect Wealth luck, and thus you are advised to build upon your savings and avoid high risk circumstances like investing heavily or a trip to the casino.

 Career

Work in 2018 may take a toll on you, as the massive pressure coupled with a harsh and inconsiderate superior might cause you to feel frequently fatigued at times. Never ending conflicts and a negative work space could also affect your competency at work. Therefore, you are encouraged to keep yourself motivated and to build your strength of character in order to push through these work obstacles. Furthermore, this may not be the best time to move jobs or positions. Although you will have to deal with this stagnation for the time being, you should try to view this situation in a more positive manner and try to stay humble and tolerant during your work tenure.

 **Relationships**

Due to the weak Peach Blossom Luck this year, it is suggested that unmarried couples put more emphasis in strengthening and maintaining their relationship. Married couple are advised to be more considerate with one another as even the simplest of misunderstandings could lead to a heated exchange between the two of you. Those of you who are still single will have to contend with being lonely for now with an inactive social lifestyle. Thus, single Dragon individuals are advised to turn their attention towards refining other aspects their life.

 **Health**

Be wary about the physical threats to your health, especially ones that come from the road. Whether you are on the sidewalk or driving a vehicle, you may potentially incur road injuries ranging from minor to fatal ones. Therefore, you are advised to strictly adhere to the road safety regulations in place at all times. Metallic objects are also a potential hazard to your health, and handlers of these objects should be careful with the rust particles it can carry. Healthy nutritional and dietary practices should also be wisely followed in order to prevent any intestinal issues from popping up.

 **Monthly Luck**

農曆正月 (February 4th - March 4th) 甲寅

Whether it is in your work or personal life, plenty of obstacles will stand in your way this month. However, if you summon your drive and energy in discovering solutions to break down these stubborn obstacles, these problems will subside and the lessons learned will better equip you to face other obstacles in your future.

農曆二月 (March 5th - April 4th) 乙卯

The Sickness Star (病符) makes its mark this month, to the detriment of your health. So to keep your health in top shape, it would be wise to exercise regularly and to obey a healthy eating diet. It is ill-advised to consume uncooked meals as it may cause you to easily fall ill. Only when your health is in prime shape can you be at your most productive and energetic.

農曆三月 (April 5th - May 4th) 丙辰

The workload you have stacked against you this month might cause you to feel weary, and thus it would be good for you to be more aware of your current work habits in order to modify them accordingly. Apart from that, a significant financial loss along with a constant barrage of disputes should alert you to be more cautious with your personal spending and attitude. Students may also substantially wane in their academic studies.

農曆四月 (May 5th - June 5th) 丁巳

This month will provide you with a good break following last month's gloomy forecast, as you will find that more things will start to smoothly go your way. So make hay while the sun shines and unleash your creativity in launching some new plans and clearing off your desk of unresolved workload.

農曆五月 (June 6th - July 6th) 戊午

Illness will befall you this month, sapping away your vigour as you try to move forward with your plans in this month. A healthy diet, consistent workout and maybe even a check-up with your physician would ensure that your health does not decline further. Moreover, the arrival of the Relief God Star (解神) will ensure a swift recovery by the month's end.

農曆六月 (July 7th - August 6th) 己未

Since the Piercing Rope Star (貫索) has a stranglehold on you this month, it is recommended that you abide by the rules and regulations in place to evade any undesirable consequences that might plague you later on. Sow diligence and consistency into your work and you will reap what is due to you.

農曆七月 (August 7th - September 7th) 庚申

The stranglehold is thankfully lifted off you this month as the auspicious Three Stages Star (三台) graces us with its presence, showering you with an abundance of luck and prosperity in your career and personal wealth. Your reputation will also get a welcome boost, so consider forging new friendships and alliances at work to witness an upturn in your work performance.

農曆八月 (September 8th - October 7th) 辛酉

This month sees the auspicious trend from last month continue to flow in your favour. Those who work may discover many opportunities to positively contribute in their given work assignments. You will be rewarded with significant cooperation and good will from your peers, superiors and clients. Also, keep an eye on your wealth prospects as it too may see a substantial growth this month. Those who are studying should expect to witness decent progress in their studies so it is advised that they hit the library and start revising. The good luck does not stop there, as single Dragon individuals are primed to potentially meet their one true love during this period.

農曆九月 (October 8th - November 6th) 壬戌

A barren month for luck this month, where it would be ill-advised to move forward with any new projects you have been cooking up to this point. You may find yourself plagued with numerous obstacles that could cause them to crumble. It would be wise for you to stay diligent and implement your creativity in completing your current workload.

農曆十月 (November 7th - December 6th) 癸亥

An encouraging month is in your midst, as good luck returns to enhance your popularity among your social circles. Therefore, hangout with your peers, spend some quality time together and your status among your friends and colleagues will improve tremendously. You might even see an upward spike in your work output as the bond between you and work peers is fortified.

農曆十一月 (December 7th 2018 - January 4th 2019) 甲子

All may seem smooth with your luck at work, but the threat of an injury will be closer than usual this month. Thus, it is highly recommended that you turn down any invitations to participate in any extreme activities that might be injurious to you. Engage in light sports and exercises to sustain a healthy lifestyle.

農曆十二月 (January 5th - February 3rd 2019) 乙丑

Luck will be a mixed bag this month due to a meeting of both auspicious and inauspicious stars. Trivial disputes with petty people will be bothersome in both your work and personal life. On the other hand, your distresses will be lifted with the appearance of a Noble Person who will aid you in conquering your hindrances and steer you to the path of improvement and righteousness. In short, although you will be initially confronted with obstacles, but the kindness and generosity of others will lift you up from that despair.

Snake 巳

Year of the Snake							
1929	1941	1953	1965	1977	1989	2001	2013

A person's Chinese age is obtained by adding one year to their Western birthday. For example, if you were born in 1976, your Western age in 2018 is 42, but your Chinese age would be 43.

Overall Forecast For The Year

巳 Aside from a few minor issues here and there, this year promises to be a good one for you so you can allow yourself to relax and enjoy the generally happy atmosphere. Your social and personal life will flourish and you will even have the chance to forge new rewarding bonds with others. While you may still run into the occasional obstacle or have a few heated disagreements with a loved one, you will not have much trouble overcoming them. With any luck, you might even find yourself in a better position than before.

Although you can expect 2018 to go smoothly for you for the most part, you will still have to be careful as the presence of the Brutal Defeat Star (暴敗) indicates that unexpected events may take place at the most inconvenient of times. These situations could throw a wrench in your carefully-laid plans and possibly even derail them outright. In order to prevent this from happening, you will have to be quick to adapt and adjust your strategy to accommodate the new element at play. Additionally, this star could affect your Wealth Luck by affecting things such as your budgets and income if you are not careful.

On a somewhat related note, another reason you should try to be more careful this year is the appearance of the Dark Sky Star (天厄) as it suggests the possibility of you getting into minor accidents. While the injuries you are likely to suffer will be minor and mostly insignificant, it would still be an inconvenience that you can avoid altogether by being more cautious and aware of your surroundings.

Aside from that, there is also the presence of the Heavenly Officer Charm Star (天官符) which could prove to be a hassle as it represents the potential for you to get into legal trouble. It is difficult to predict how such issues could manifest in your life although there is a strong likelihood that they could stem from the aforementioned hiccups in your plans.

This could also tie into the influence of the Death God Star (亡神) which suggests that you could end up embroiled in arguments over trivial matters and accidentally offend someone. Something like this may snowball into more serious issues and lead to you suffering severe consequences for your actions. In light of this, it is strongly recommended that you choose your words carefully and control your emotions whenever you interact with others. You will find it easier to avoid getting into trouble if you have a clear and calm mind.

However, there is no need for you to worry yourself too much about all this as there are other stars present which will counteract or mitigate these undesirable situations. The biggest sign in favour of this optimistic outlook is the Dragon Virtue Star (龍德) which heralds good omens and an overall sense of positivity. Expect to hear snippets of good news on a frequent enough basis and look forward to being able to experience many happy occasions. In fact, your luck may be so good that you will be able to successfully deal with any problems that arise and even potentially turn things around in your favour.

Additionally, there is the Emperor Star (紫微) which suggests that your relationships with others will only flourish and grow stronger during this period. It also indicates that you can expect Noble people in your life especially in your hour of need. These individuals along with your family and friends will be there to help and guide you when you find yourself in a tough situation. With their assistance, you will be able to maintain happiness as well as achieve the goals you have set for yourself.

Your personal life will also flourish throughout this year thanks to the Red Matchmaker Star (紅鸞) which will have an immensely positive impact on your social activities. Its energies will facilitate your ability to meet new people as well as form close and rewarding connections with them. Those of you who are single will be particularly thrilled as this star is very conducive for finding love. Meanwhile, those who are in committed relationships will be able to strengthen their bonds and may even want to consider taking the next step. Married couples can also enjoy the romantic vibes this star emits by spending more quality time together.

The Forecast for Individual Aspects of the Year

 **Wealth**

2018 brings a lot of uncertainty in terms of your financial wealth. In the beginning, you might incur some monetary losses, possibly due to failed investment projects or excessive gambling habits. However, you will soon be able to recuperate your earlier losses through the guidance of several compassionate individuals. If you generously accept the help provided to you, this year will ultimately be a rewarding one for your wealth.

 Career

It is advisable that you initially focus your efforts on reshuffling your career priorities. You could do this by either moving to a different job position or a different company altogether. Once you have managed to stabilize your work life, you can start to carefully conceptualise some grander plans for the year ahead. Slowly but surely, you will eventually be able to execute these plans successfully. The second half of the year will see a sharp boost in your luck prospects. Therefore, you might want to utilize this period to reenergise your work performance for the rest of the year.

蛇

The Snake in 2018

 Relationships

Whether you are single or in a relationship, 2018 is the year for you to improve your relationship prospects significantly. Those of you who are still single could finally find yourselves in a fruitful relationship with the right person. Therefore, single Snakes should initiate the search for a potential partner during the year. Unmarried couples who are in a devoted relationship should become engaged as soon as possible to usher in a long and prosperous marriage. On the other hand, couples who have already exchanged their marital vows might want to restrain their potentially amorous feelings towards others outside of the marriage. Doing this could avoid a marital breakdown that might be caused by you or your partner potentially engaging in extramarital affairs.

 **Health**

Your health is of paramount importance in 2018, especially for senior citizens. Elderly people might be visiting the hospital more often than they would have liked as a result of being afflicted by some ailments. Thus, those in their golden years should pay attention to their physician's medical advice, observe a healthy diet and take the prescribed medications to maintain their well-being. They should immediately make an appointment with their doctor should they experience any stomach or intestinal problems to prevent it from becoming worse.

 **Monthly Luck**

農曆正月 (February 4th - March 4th) 甲寅

The lunar year kicks off with an air of positivity as this month ushers in an abundance of aid and guidance into your work life. Good-natured colleagues will provide you with some much needed advice in terms of your job performance. Your superiors might also lend you a helping hand in alleviating some of the workload from you. Accept this generosity with open arms and gratitude, and your month will turn out well.

農曆二月 (March 5th - April 4th) 乙卯

Your energy levels could be noticeably depleted this year, with a sudden swell of work assignments and business meetings taking up most of your precious time. Do your best to remain motivated by putting in the hard-work required to tackle the responsibilities at hand. Sooner or later, your diligence might be duly repaid with a grateful gesture from your superiors in the form of a salary bonus.

農曆三月 (April 5th - May 4th) 丙辰

Several joyful occasions will occur this month and you could be in store for a pleasant surprise. It could be a sought-after promotion or a cheerful family affair regarding the birth of a new family member. As jubilant as these events might be, it is wise to always exercise a fair amount of restraint and alertness in your celebrations to avoid certain spiteful individuals from disrupting the festivities.

農曆四月 (May 5th - June 5th) 丁巳

Due to the presence of the Grand Duke Star (太歲), be sure to exercise even more caution than last month. This is mainly due to the heightened risks of road accidents. From sidewalks to vehicles, every section of the street presents its own unique hazards that you should be wary of. It is imperative that you adhere to the road regulations when crossing the street or driving on the road. Furthermore, plan your schedule wisely as this month. You could be spending a long time away from your loved ones due to work commitments.

農曆五月 (June 6th - July 6th) 戊午

Obstacles in your personal and career life could impede some of the progress that you have been making this month. However, with the Sun Star (太陽) on your side during this period, the steady flow of difficulties into your life will be quickly diminished to welcome a relatively peaceful phase for the rest of the month.

農曆六月 (July 7th - August 6th) 己未

This month is highly inauspicious as you will be confronted with many hurdles to overcome. You will not only encounter a growing workload and higher expectations from your superiors, but also an absence of help from your colleagues. You are going to need to buckle up and work hard on the solutions to figure out these problems and get through the month with optimism.

農曆七月 (August 7th - September 7th) 庚申

After a previously turbulent month, an auspicious period arrives this month with several cheerful events to relax your mind and body. The time is ripe for you to make some momentous headway in your planned endeavours in order to see it come into fruition. As Peach Blossom Luck appears this month, single Snake individuals can look out for a potential partner to begin a relationship with. Moreover, Snake couples should expect a relatively stable bond with little to no relationship issues.

農曆八月 (September 8th - October 7th) 辛酉

A timely boost to your reputation should enhance your popularity and conversational prowess among your wider social circle. This will increase your connection and bond with your friends and colleagues. Thus, you might receive some much needed assistance from people whom you had previously considered as an acquaintance.

農曆九月 (October 8th - November 6th) 壬戌

You might experience a slight financial loss as this month rolls in. Although control over these circumstances might be out of your hands for the time being, you can mitigate the situation from further losses through prudent financial planning. You can also consider taking a nobler route by making charitable contributions for a cause you intensely support.

農曆十月 (November 7th - December 6th) 癸亥

Inauspicious stars from last month will continue to beset you both in your family and work life. Not only could you be bogged down by a hefty workload, but your consistent efforts to produce meaningful work results will go unnoticed by your superiors as well. You might also unintentionally cause a rift between you and your life partner or family members. This household dilemma could further add to your frustrations during this period. Practice patience in your interactions with your superiors and family members so that you do not aggravate these discords even further.

農曆十一月 (December 7th 2018 - January 4th 2019) 甲子

After experiencing a couple of months of unfavourable luck, your fortunes will finally change for the better this month. The presence of Indirect Wealth indicates a potential increase of wealth in your favour, possibly in the form a fruitful investment or rewarding side job. While you might be seeing your finances prosper, refrain from purchasing large amounts of assets which could decrease your wealth significantly.

農曆十二月 (January 5th - February 3rd 2019) 乙丑

Prosperity still favours you this month, so dedicate yourself to engaging in any creative plans that you may have been previously holding back on. The additional affluence this month will also see you achieve your desired goals with resounding success. While you are at it, arrange your schedule to include more family time and your harmonious relationship with your family will bring more happiness.

Horse 午

Year of the Horse							
1930	1942	1954	1966	1978	1990	2002	2014

A person's Chinese age is obtained by adding one year to their Western birthday. For example, if you were born in 1976, your Western age in 2018 is 42, but your Chinese age would be 43.

Overall Forecast For The Year

午 2018 will be a blast for you with the presence of three favourable stars. You will find yourself surrounded by generous and supportive people, and standing at the forefront to receive the best of good fortune when wealth opportunities open up. What's more, you will gain an extra edge on solving any conflicts and issues should they arise. You seem to have it all in the new year!

Blessed by the General Star (將星) in the upcoming year, you will be able to receive assistance from kind and sincere people when you are in need; they will also offer you strength and support when you are feeling a little dragged down by the rapid changes that may happen. But you should not be overly-cautious with any changes that occur this new year, for they will most likely bring positive influences into your life, especially in regards to your wealth.

Also present is the Golden Lock Star (金匱) that indicates wealth and financial gain. The star discovers and locks in golden opportunities for you to accumulate wealth, so you may see great potentials in the new year to earn a pay raise, receive bonuses for hard work, and increase business profit margins. Be on the lookout for lucrative investments in property or in shares, which you may get good reliable tips from your social circle, and watch your asset multiply in this prosperous year. It will be a great year to lay a strong foundation for your future.

The icing on the cake is the presence of the Earth Relief (地解) Star in the coming year, which indicates that you will possess the skills required to solve almost any issues and the ability to turn the tables in your favour. This auspicious star backing you up will shield you from the effects of other negative stars present, and guide you to find positive resolution to any conflict you face. With the aid of the Earth Relief, and the generous blessings of the General and the Golden Lock Stars, there is no reason you should hold back from pursuing your goals this new year.

However, you should only charge forward in full force after carefully consider every step of your plans. The presence of the Great Sha Star (大煞) indicates high risk of financial loss and damage to reputation if you make impulsive decisions. Good strategy and ample preparation will guarantee you better chances at succeeding. Think thoroughly in any dealings, and avoid gambling on things you have not understood inside out. Obtain all related information before you sign any papers; consider all possible consequences of your actions. Get to the details of everything, and you will be able to make the most of the new year without burning a hole in your pocket.

While you are on the top of your game, you should also watch your words and actions, as the White Tiger (白虎) and the Sky Warrior (天雄) Stars indicate the possibility of accidents and communication difficulties. Take precautions when you travel and undertake physical activities; remember to not push yourself over your own limits. You should also try to be considerate when you speak. Stepping into others' shoes before you speak will help you to voice your thoughts and opinions in a way that others will be more willing to listen and accept.

As you focus on your career and social network, you should not neglect your family in 2018. This is because a member in the family or household may require your attention, as indicated by the presence of the Pealing Head Star (披頭). The star increases the risk of a family member having some health condition, so pay extra care to your family if anyone seems to be feeling under the weather. It is also good to spend more quality time with your family.

You have the opportunities and support to aim for the stars and be the top dog position in the Year of Dog. Staying focused and be thorough with your plans enable you to avoid pitfalls and potential delays in your undertakings. If you have it all figured out, go on and ride a wave of good luck and popularity in 2018; you will be unstoppable!

The Forecast for Individual Aspects of the Year

 **Wealth**

2018 is a fantastic year in regards to your wealth. You will experience a wealth surge primarily from the support of your generous friends and peers, so be sure to receive this aid with gratitude. An excellent turn in your work performance will also see more doors of opportunity open to you, providing you with a platform to achieve a business profit or salary increase this year.

 Career

Tread carefully at work as conflicts may arise between you and your colleagues which might prove to be disadvantageous for you. You may not see eye to eye on certain topics and your peers at work might isolate you due to these differences in opinions. Be wary at all times as someone might be plotting to backstab you when you least expect it. To remedy this situation, strengthen the bond between you and those you work with by attending more social events together and practice open and effective communication.

 **Relationships**

Unmarried couples should consider tying the knot this year in order to significantly boost the strength of their companionship. For single Horses, even with the absence of the Peach Blossom Luck, there still might be a good chance for you to get into a relationship. Thus, those who are single should take a calculated leap of faith and profess their love to the one they adore. The chances of you being in a romantic relationship could be good this year.

 **Health**

There will be a threat of risky events on the road, whether you are inside or outside a vehicle. Ensure you follow traffic rules to avoid the possibility of road accidents as much as possible in this coming year. In addition to that, metallic objects should always be handled with care and consideration as these items could seriously bring you harm. Observe a healthy diet and exercise frequently to prevent any digestive problems from showing up.

 **Monthly Luck**

農曆正月 (February 4th - March 4th) 甲寅

Obstacles will pervasive from all sides this month, whether it is in your work or personal life. You might find it difficult to connect intimately with certain family members and it may seem that all your efforts to lessen your workload are unfruitful. As exhausting as it may seem, practise due diligence and consistency in all aspects of your life and these issues will eventually clear away.

農曆二月 (March 5th - April 4th) 乙卯

An auspicious month dawns on you, so get the most out of this tranquil period and exercise your creativity by designing unique plans to achieve the goals you have set out for this year. Luck in love is also in the picture, so muster the courage to confess your true feelings to that person you are interested in and you might end up in a loving long-term relationship.

農曆三月 (April 5th - May 4th) 丙辰

Caution should be observed as the Heavenly Dog Star (天狗) enters this month. You will have to stay on your toes as you will be faced with tricky obstacles. The onus will be on you to be level-headed about it as you attempt to generate innovative solutions to resolve these obstacles blocking your way.

農曆四月 (May 5th - June 5th) 丁巳

Like last month, this month also warrants caution, especially because it pertains to your health. A visit from the Sickness Star (病符) might bring along various illnesses and injuries if you are not careful. Good food hygiene and plenty of light physical activities would help to avert much of these unpleasant possibilities.

農曆五月 (June 6th - July 6th) 戊午

An abundance of obstacles might be the last thing you would have been looking forward to this month, but nonetheless you are advised to brace yourself as you will be bogged down by inconsequential arguments and fights with petty people. These state of affairs might escalate to the point where you might be embroiled in legal entanglements. You should heighten your senses in preparation for what might transpire.

農曆六月 (July 7th - August 6th) 己未

This month you will discover work to proceed smoothly as you start to hit all your targets. Your superiors may even outwardly display their appreciation for your work efforts. Colleagues will also find satisfaction while working alongside you as your approval rating gets a timely boost. Additionally, your personal life will see a favourable upturn as single Horse individuals on the hunt for their life partner may find their efforts bearing fruit.

農曆七月 (August 7th - September 7th) 庚申

Prepare your mind and body for a hectic month ahead as your schedule will be packed with travelling either for your personal or professional obligations. Therefore, fatigue might set in during this time and the end of this month might see your pockets lighter than usual. Mitigate this by maintaining an exercise regime as you move about and plan your travel budget in advance.

農曆八月 (September 8th - October 7th) 辛酉

Good fortune will be prevalent this month in almost all key facets of your life. Deadlines will be met with ease and your workload might be lighter this time around as you pour the necessary effort into it. If you are single, you might be in an opportune stage to make your true feelings known to that special someone you truly adore. Couples should keep their interactions with other people in check to avoid any misunderstandings later on.

農曆九月 (October 8th - November 6th) 壬戌

The uptrend from last month continues into this month, although it might not be as strong. Small hurdles will be found along your path but as long you find the motivation to discover the solutions to these matters, you will overcome these hurdles with ease and the rest of the month is yours to relish.

農曆十月 (November 7th - December 6th) 癸亥

As the Moon Virtue Star (月德) emerges this month, your career will be blessed with good fortune and progress in many areas of your work. Your workload will see a remarkable decrease in volume and the targets you set for yourself will be met with relative ease. Moreover, your colleagues and superiors will rally behind you to demonstrate their support for your accomplishments.

農曆十一月 (December 7th 2018 - January 4th 2019) 甲子

Previous months of good fortune will come to an abrupt end this month. This means that increasing amount of hindrances might appear in your life to disrupt your agendas. Maturity is crucial to carefully tackle these obstacles as it might eventually alleviate some of the distress.

農曆十二月 (January 5th - February 3rd 2019) 乙丑

Fortunately, this lunar year closes out in your favour in every venture you seek to face this month as opposed to last month's misery. Get those creative gears in your mind grinding to discover new ideas and design new solutions. You might usher in some personal life improvements. A Noble Person will also be present in your life to lend a helping hand whenever you might need it.

Goat 未

Year of the Goat							
1931	1943	1955	1967	1979	1991	2003	2015

A person's Chinese age is obtained by adding one year to their Western birthday. For example, if you were born in 1976, your Western age in 2018 is 42, but your Chinese age would be 43.

The Goat in 2018

羊

Overall Forecast For The Year

Look forward to 2018 as it promises to be a year dominated primarily by good tidings and positive events. Although you will have to contend with a few trials and tribulations every now and then, none of them will be serious or significant enough to cause you much trouble in the long run. Whatever form these inconveniences may take, you can rest assured as you will have the help you need to overcome them as well as the golden opportunities to make up for them.

Perhaps the most obvious positive change in your life during this period will be the appearance of individuals who can give you a helping hand in some way or another thanks to the influence of the Nobleman Star (貴人). The Noble people that this star will draw into your life will take a variety of forms from mentors to random benevolent souls that happen to be at the right place at the right time to assist you. With these individuals' help, any trouble you run into will be made significantly more manageable, less stressful and easy to deal with.

Complementing this will be the effects of the Prosperity Star (福星) which suggests that you will be able to enjoy seeing some progress being made in terms of your efforts to advance your career. Because of this abundance of positive energies emanating from both stars, you will likely find yourself being presented with more than a few opportunities to showcase your talents and get noticed by your superiors. All you need to do is make full use of every chance available to you and it will be more than possible for you to secure a pay raise, hefty bonus or even a promotion for yourself.

You may also find some advantage with the presence of the Jade Hall Star (玉堂) which signifies an excellent time for asset acquisition aside from engaging in activities relating to financial and business matters involving assets. If you are looking to increase your wealth this year, you will definitely find favour from the positive influence of this star which will also be supportive in any effort to shore up your finances.

Unfortunately, the achievements and success that you will have to your name are also likely to produce some unwanted consequences in the process. Thanks to the presence of both the Curled Tongue (卷舌) and Crossing Sha (絞煞) Stars, there is a possibility of you having to deal with malicious lies thrown your way by those envious of your accomplishments. Additionally, these unscrupulous individuals could try to pick fights with you and embroil you in pointless disputes. Some of your existing relationships may also sour as a result of this atmosphere or jealousy and animosity. In light of all this, it would be in your best interest to ignore these people and stay focused on your work.

There is also the Triple Punishment Star (三刑) present which brings with it the implication that you could end up butting heads with your family members from time to time, throughout the year. The issues that trigger these clashes and disputes are likely to range from trivial to serious in nature. Nevertheless, it is very important that you always keep in mind that the bonds you have with these people are priceless and not worth destroying over a mere disagreement. You should therefore do your best to remain calm and reasonable during these arguments so that a peaceful resolution can be found.

Luckily for you, the Heavenly Virtue Star (天德) will also be present and can help to mitigate the aforementioned negative events. Its positive energies will give your problem-solving abilities a much-needed boost, something which will definitely come in handy when dealing with something potentially volatile. This star's effects on your life also tie into those of the Nobleman star as it indicates that you will receive the assistance you need from your family, friends and colleagues. This is a clear sign that no matter what differences of opinion you may have with those around you, they will still come to your aid when you need them.

One aspect of your life which will need your full attention is your well-being due to the influence of the Yellow Flag Star (黃幡). While it does not suggest that you will experience a significant health scare sometime this year, you should still not take your health for granted. Even if you happen to be in peak physical condition right now, you are encouraged to maintain a healthy lifestyle and see a doctor the moment you suspect something is amiss.

There is also the Lonesome Star's (寡宿) presence to take into consideration as it can affect your mental and emotional health. As its name implies, you could feel lonely and unwanted possibly due to your situation at work or the arguments you may be having with your loved ones. In order to prevent these emotions from overwhelming you, it is advisable that you confide in someone you can trust and not bottle it up.

The Forecast for Individual Aspects of the Year

 **Wealth**

Amidst your hectic work schedule and the increasing workload on your desk, this is the year for you to shift your main focus into increasing your monetary wealth. Do not let the demands of work distract you from looking into other opportunities that might significantly improve your financial standing. Those of you who are working in the clerical domain may receive the brunt of your work assignments from hopping in between various work settings, so take careful notice of the amount of workload you will receive this year in order to appropriately manage your responsibilities.

 **Career**

Collaboration with the opposite sex is the key to a progressive career outlook in 2018, so set aside any personal notions you may have of the opposite sex. Be open to their ideas and thoughts to obtain highly favourable work prospects. Continue to motivate yourself to strive for more achievements in your career and opportunities, and showcasing your hidden talents will benefit you in the long run. All in all, 2018 marks a fruitful year where your diligence and persistence at work will be duly rewarded.

 **Relationships**

Ladies in particular are forecasted to experience weaker luck prospects in romantic relationships as opposed to men due to the weak Peach Blossom Luck in 2018. Thus, ladies are advised to place more emphasis in the development of other facets in their life while single men can look forward to discovering their one true life partner by mingling within their current social circles. Stable couples who are planning to tie the knot should initiate plans to be married. Married couples may want to tread carefully with their feelings for others outside of their marriage as this sensitive issue may lead to relationship issues in the future.

Health

Your wealth is in health this year as your body and mind will be in prime condition to tackle 2018 with dynamism and vigour. Therefore, hitting the gym, learning a new sport, practising a healthy diet and observing personal safety are all activities that you could dive into in order to equip yourself for a year free of major diseases and physical afflictions.

Monthly Luck

農曆正月 (February 4th - March 4th) 甲寅

This month may see several disputes, ranging from trivial bouts to court litigations, pop up on your radar. Adhering to the standard rules and regulations in place at all times will help you avoid these troubled waters. Other than that, this month looks to be filled with joyous occasions that will uplift your spirits and stir your confidence.

農曆二月 (March 5th - April 4th) 乙卯

As the auspicious Three Combinations Star (三合) arrives this month, you may look forward to a smooth period without any hiccups, so grab this chance to reduce your work pile and to realise your newly conceived ideas. Also, your finances will experience an upsurge in terms of your savings, so adjust your budget to maximise this monetary inflow. Those in academic circles can anticipate a smooth studying phase from their tests revisions to attainment of new skills.

農曆三月 (April 5th - May 4th) 丙辰

Auspicious and inauspicious stars cross paths this month resulting in mixed outlooks for you. As such, you may find it difficult to predict when a bad storm or a good omen is on your horizon. Although you may feel that the control over your fate is out of your hands, endure through it with determination and preparation and you should see out this month amicably.

農曆四月 (May 5th - June 5th) 丁巳

Good fortune has landed on your shores this month, so take a breather and enjoy this relaxing period of uneventful stability. Not much may transpire during this time, but those in the clerical and academic field may look forward to a favourable stroke of good fortune in their work and academic output.

農曆五月 (June 6th - July 6th) 戊午

Get ready to be invigorated this month with the arrival of more auspicious luck. Putting in the right amounts of effort will yield you lucrative work outcomes as the tide of goodwill is flowing concurrently with your work progress. Cooperation with your colleagues is encouraged as you will be remunerated with abundant success in your endeavour.

農曆六月 (July 7th - August 6th) 己未

Taking a sharp 180-degree turn from the previous month, an inauspicious omen will affect your life as decisions concerning your work and personal life are not likely to have favourable outcomes. Your efforts will go unappreciated by your superiors as you barely scrape by your deadlines. Hence, prepare your course of action by carefully examining the consequences of any decision you are going to make to avoid any regrettable outcomes later.

農曆七月 (August 7th - September 7th) 庚申

As the Lonesome Star (孤辰) reveals itself to you this month, loneliness will take centre stage in your personal life as your loved ones fall lower on your priorities in favour of growing work commitments. Likewise, your family members and friends will also sense this emotional isolation from you, much to their disappointment. Manage your time effectively to try and stay connected with the ones close to you.

農曆八月 (September 8th - October 7th) 辛酉

You will have to contend with some unfavourable luck this month. Unpleasant surprises may be revealed in various aspects of your life, so be always wary of them as they occur. However, the Relief God Star (解神) will bring some respite from the misery that these obstacles bring and put you on track to achieve your desired goals.

農曆九月 (October 8th - November 6th) 壬戌

Pass up on high risk activities this month due to the heightened risk serious injuries. Vigilance to your surroundings is key. It is advisable that you refrain from plunging head first into anything that might require extreme physical effort. Little hitches might befall you from time to time but it will not have any significant detrimental effect on you.

農曆十月 (November 7th - December 6th) 癸亥

It's going to be great month for you in both your work and personal life, so be productive at work and strive towards improving your personal bonds with your loved ones. Single Goat individuals should prudently keep their hearts opened as they are primed to meet that special someone that they have been searching for in their social circles. Nights out might be a potential hazard for you so instead enjoy the company of your family and friends indoors.

農曆十一月 (December 7th 2018 - January 4th 2019) 甲子

A slightly unfavourable month here might cause you to lose a sum of money. However, it will not significantly hurt your pocket and tedious financial management will ensure no more money than necessary is lost.

農曆十二月 (January 5th - February 3rd 2019) 乙丑

The end of the lunar year requires you to be highly aware of the state of your personal finances and health as those aspects may take a downward turn this month. Therefore, a healthy lifestyle through exercising and eating sufficiently and refraining yourself from any hefty investment is highly advisable.

Monkey 申

Year of the Monkey							
1932	1944	1956	1968	1980	1992	2004	2016

A person's Chinese age is obtained by adding one year to their Western birthday. For example, if you were born in 1976, your Western age in 2018 is 42, but your Chinese age would be 43.

Overall Forecast For The Year

申 2018 could prove to be a rather trying year for you and you will have to find the strength within you to persevere and still triumph over the challenges you encounter. These difficulties are likely to manifest in both your personal and professional lives but they will not be anything that you cannot handle as long as you maintain the right mind-set. Aside from that, you may also have to contend with financial instability and tumultuous relationships. Your well-being is yet another thing that you will have to keep an eye on especially when it comes to your emotional health.

One of the things that you will have to carefully monitor throughout this period is your finances as your Wealth Luck during this time does not look particularly rosy. There is a chance that your expenditures could outpace your income if you are not careful. This is where budgeting and carefully managing your expenses will come in extremely useful. If you think that you have the time and energy to spare, you may also want to consider getting a secondary source of income to supplement your main one.

On that note, there is a chance that you may not see your career advance much and work might not go as smoothly as you would like. There are likely to be quite a few obstacles popping up as you try to do your job and this could have a profound effect on your productivity levels in terms of speed and efficiency. In order to avoid or at the very least mitigate this situation, you will have to work twice as hard as usual. Try to prepare as many contingencies as possible and do not get discouraged when you run into trouble. With any luck, you will be able to not only make it through this tough time in one piece but also prove to your superiors that you are a valuable employee.

However, there may actually be a golden opportunity to bolster this part of your life thanks to the Sky Horse Star (天馬). Its presence in your life suggests that you may be in for an extensive travelling stint as a result of your job. You should embrace this chance as there is a strong possibility that it will give you a valuable advantage when it comes to advancing your career.

The potential benefits of this trip may not be apparent to you immediately but they will almost certainly pay off in the long run. Alternatively, those who are still studying will be similarly affected by this star and may find themselves travelling somewhere far away to further their education. With the Literary Arts Star (文昌) in place, this may be especially true for such individuals. Those who are in the business of learning, research and academia will not only find more opportunities this year, but will also find their endeavours yield results in the form of tangible results and significant breakthroughs.

Regardless, there is one potential source of concern which you should take seriously this year and that is your health. This is especially true when it comes to your emotional and mental health due to the influence of the Sky Cry Star (天哭) which may make you more sensitive and easily affected by the events around you. Due to your potentially heightened emotional state, you may find yourself prone to suffering from anxiety and a general feeling of uneasiness. It is important that you do not let yourself be consumed by all these negative emotions as this will only hamper your ability to deal with the problems that caused them in the first place. Do not be afraid to confide in your loved ones and ask them for their help when you need it.

There is also the possibility of you getting into an accident when travelling on the road or taking part in high-risk activities so make sure you follow all safety precautions in both situations. On a related note, married individuals may want to keep an eye on their spouse's well-being as their health could also suffer during this period. Both of you should endeavour to play it safe this year and avoid dangerous undertakings such as extreme sports. A healthy diet and non-strenuous exercise routine would also work wonders.

On a somewhat related note, it would be advisable if you refrained from attending any funerals this year. This is because of the combined presence of the Sky Dog (天狗) and Funeral Guest (吊客) Stars which indicate that if you do end up going to such events, the negative energies that are so prevalent in such situations will have a noticeable and negative impact on your own well-being. If there is a funeral and you can opt out, it would be in your best interest to do so.

The Forecast for Individual Aspects of the Year

 **Wealth**

Financial matters might take an inauspicious turn this year with more money exiting than entering it due to unrestricted spending. Sensible purchases and a lot of more self-control on luxurious items at the start of 2018 might offset some of the monetary loss you may experience later on. It is highly advisable that you plan your financial budget effectively and avoid any high-risk activities in order to minimise your spending and maximise your savings.

 Career

Expect to encounter a seemingly endless stream of obstacles and disputes in your career this year. Your superiors will be difficult to please and you might barely meet your deadlines as they come which will naturally stunt your work progress as the year goes by. Strive to be diligent and relentless in your work assignments and be generous in your interactions with your colleagues and superiors and soon enough you will find headway in your overall work output.

 **Relationships**

Weak Peach Blossom Luck in 2018 spells an undesirable relationship outlook for those who are still single. Single Monkey individuals should therefore adjust their romantic expectations wisely in order to avoid any disappointments. Health should be the main focus for married and unmarried couples as you or your partner are more prone to illnesses and injuries this year. Couples should pay careful attention to any possible health issues and it is recommended that a team effort from both parties is necessary to keep each other free of health issues, perhaps by joining a gender-inclusive gym class or cooking healthy meals together. It may provide an opportunity to foster better intimacy between couples.

 **Health**

Be on the alert for your health this year as your physical well-being may take a hit due to possible light or heavy injuries, especially on the road. Thus, obeying the standard traffic rules will go a long way in keeping yourself safe from physical harm. Also, try to avoid participating in extreme sports if you have not adequately prepared any essential safety measures beforehand. Hazards at work are also a possibility, so always be wary of any assignments or relationships which may present a physical risk to reduce any harmful effects it could have on your well-being.

Monthly Luck

農曆正月 (February 4th - March 4th) 甲寅

The lunar year kicks off with a month full of complications that might put a halt to all the development at work. Certain moments might even seem to place you in a do or die predicament as you find yourself facing a mountainous workload. Formulate your decisions effectively to minimize the challenges you will be undergoing this month.

農曆二月 (March 5th - April 4th) 乙卯

Some obstacles from last month may remain and new ones may pop up this month, but do not worry as these challenges would prove to be easier to surmount as the month goes on. Other than that, a positive outlook is in store for you with your finances finally bearing fruit, your work producing the results you desire and your family can see more of you as you will acquire more time to spend with them.

農曆三月 (April 5th - May 4th) 丙辰

Rejoice as your luck this month will experience a dramatic upturn from last month's already relatively optimistic perspective. Your career and wealth will continue its meteoric rise in scope and development in the form of a salary bonus or a promotion. Your household will continue to remain harmonious as the bonds between you and your family members grow.

農曆四月 (May 5th - June 5th) 丁巳

Keeping with the run of good luck you are experiencing the previous two months, this month continues to with an auspicious forecast in regards to your career prospects. A tremendous boost to your wealth will occur as you calmly excel in your work environment. Plus, a window of opportunities will present itself to you as a Noble Person arrives to help steady the course of your career.

農曆五月 (June 6th - July 6th) 戊午

This month signals the fourth month in a row for your auspicious streak. So get ready for a relatively smooth month ahead with little to no bumps along the way. Those in the secretarial line can look forward to outstanding results in their job which could garner significant attention from your superiors and colleagues. Academic students may anticipate a period of attaining new skills that could aid in their studies and examinations. Parents itching to enrol their children into a new institution or programme should begin executing their plans in this month.

農曆六月 (July 7th - August 6th) 己未

Your four-month period of bountiful luck comes to an abrupt end this month as there is a high chance that sickness might befall you. Keep to a healthy physical routine and distance yourself from fatty and oily foods. This will at least ensure to some degree that bad health be kept at bay. If you are single, keep your eyes peeled for any opportunities to mingle in a social setting with someone you adore and a rewarding relationship could blossom out of it.

農曆七月 (August 7th - September 7th) 庚申

A trying month is expected ahead as you will encounter increasing demands in your personal and professional life. Intense family matters and a swell of workload on your plate could occupy most of your time and energy as you try to stay on top of these circumstances. However, the rest of the month will not overwhelm you completely and you should be riding out the month in a smooth fashion.

農曆八月 (September 8th - October 7th) 辛酉

Fewer obstructions will appear this month although you will be required to portray a steadfast attitude and a persistent determination to overcome them effectively. A Noble Person will also come to your aid to help overcome these barriers which block your progress at work and in your personal life. Be open with accepting their assistance when they enter your life.

農曆九月 **(October 8th - November 6th)** 壬戌

This month will bring you fresh new challenges for you to overcome. Proceed ahead with a clear head and maintain vigilance or you end up making decisions that might not work out great for you. Furthermore, open yourself up to new ideas and solutions along the way as the answers to your problems could come from a fresh perspective.

農曆十月 **(November 7th - December 6th)** 癸亥

Your health should be of utmost importance this month as significant harm might be looming around the corner. Therefore, you should give a pass on high-risk sports for the moment and instead focus on implementing some precautions when it comes to any physical activity you might be involved in. Exercise caution at work as well since the busy schedules and huge work piles may eventually take a toll on your health and productivity.

農曆十一月 **(December 7th 2018 - January 4th 2019)** 甲子

Auspicious stars appear for you this month with plenty of opportunities to positively highlight your work performance and talents presenting themselves to you. You are encouraged to grab these opportunities whenever you can to impress your superiors and clients at work and it could result in a healthy return of wealth and job prospects in your favour.

農曆十二月 **(January 5th - February 3rd 2019)** 乙丑

As the year comes to end, this month ensures that you will continue to revel in the good fortune from the previous month. Potential investors should not miss this chance to grow their investment portfolio with fresh new ventures while those looking to cultivate their career path can begin to formulate their next steps in advancing their job prospects. In addition, be on the lookout for a joyous event that could impact your life for the better.

Rooster 酉

Year of the Rooster							
1933	1945	1957	1969	1981	1993	2005	2017

A person's Chinese age is obtained by adding one year to their Western birthday. For example, if you were born in 1976, your Western age in 2018 is 42, but your Chinese age would be 43.

Overall Forecast For The Year

The previous year has most likely been eventful for you, leaving you feeling a little exhausted and burnt out. The new year 2018 will arrive just in time to offer you the breather you may have been anticipating. 2018 will let you slow down and recharge yourself, by giving you the opportunity to review, examine and change your lifestyle to a better one. If your well-being has not been your priority, the coming year will encourage you to find a healthy balance in life and take better care of yourself, both physically and emotionally.

The stars accompanying you in the Year of Dog will help you to evaluate your lifestyle and keep your work-life balance in-check. With the presence of the Mo Yue Star (陌越), there is a tendency to be anxious or agitated. If you have been working very hard and neglecting your health in the process, the star will serve to remind you of the importance of maintaining a healthy balance between your work and your well-being. When you don't allow yourself to rest and your emotional needs be taken care of, you tend to get worked up by small things, and that will not benefit you in climbing the corporate ladder or winning a career advancement.

Although the Mo Yue Star indicates mental and emotional anguish, it is unlikely that your concerns or troubles in the coming year will have any real impact in your life, unless you allow them to take form in your mind and affect your otherwise clear and sound judgement. You should know better to let trivial things get to you in this new year. When someone at work gives you the cold shoulder, it does not mean he or she dislikes you; perhaps their minds are simply preoccupied by other things. Learn to distinguish between unfounded doubts and real threats, as well as to let go of hurtful feelings. You care a lot about how others see you, but you also have to look after yourself. Regular meditation may help you to clear your thoughts and emotions, refreshing and revitalising your mind.

The effect of the Mo Yue Star is also amplified by the presence of the Six Harms Star (六害). The name of this star may sound threatening, but the threats it poses are most likely merely empty threats in your own head. The Six Harms Star suggests feelings of loneliness and isolation; however, these anxieties are not necessary a true reflection of the situation you are in. Just like the Mo Yue Star, the Six Harms Star reminds you the need for a reality check if you find yourself in mental agony. Fears that you have been abandoned or there is no support available are most probably not true. Do not let these fears grow in you; instead, go out, get some fresh air, talk to your friends, family and mentors, and you will find yourself more grounded and connected to the reality.

Mental anguish may only be in your head, but the presence of the Sickness Charm Star (病符) denotes the possibility of real physical illness. If you have not been taking good care of your own health, the coming year may see some health setbacks to remind you to put priorities in place. Health is wealth; if you do not maintain a healthy body, you will not have the capacity to enjoy the rewards of your hard labour. Without good health, your work performance may be deterred as well. Therefore, staying healthy and at the top of your game should be your first priority. Make sure you get enough rest and eat healthily; your body will thank you for taking care of it.

2018 will be the perfect time for you to improve yourself in terms of well-being. There may be fears and doubts at times, but as the saying goes, there is nothing to be feared but fear itself; conquer your fears and you will see that things aren't that bad as you thought. Learn to put your own well-being before anything else this new year, and start instituting healthy lifestyle choices such as eating clean, exercising regularly and meditating from time to time. By the end of 2018, you will find yourself renewed and refreshed!

The Forecast for Individual Aspects of the Year

 **Wealth**

This year's financial outlook should be tackled with caution as you could suffer a significant loss. Therefore, in the beginning of the year, it is highly recommended that you start purchasing assets, which would not likely depreciate in value as the year goes by, in order to symbolise good cash expenditure. Take heart at the fact that the presence of Indirect Wealth means you will benefit greatly from some side income.

 Career

A number of impediments could stall your career progression in 2018. A burgeoning amount of work and pressure could place you in an undesirable position this year. Although you may wish to begin planning some new projects to advance your career prospects, it is better to stick to the current tasks at hand. Practice determination and hard work in everything that is thrown at you for the time being. In addition, welcome the opportunities to travel for work purposes. The lessons you will learn from these experiences will aid you in producing more refined work results. Moreover, the additional assistance you will receive from your friends will ensure a relatively smooth career outlook this year.

 **Relationships**

The Peach Blossom Luck in 2018 marks its presence, to the benefit of those who are single and who are already in a relationship. Single Rooster individuals should take the initiative to mingle in their social circles more often to find that special someone. Couples who are currently considering marriage should take a leap of faith and execute plans for a wedding ceremony this year. Married Rooster individuals will be greeted with multiple joyous moments in their family, possibly ushering a new child into the household.

 **Health**

Keep a watchful eye over your health this year as fatigue and illnesses will be particularly troubling throughout the calendar year. Do not worry because should you fall ill, the presence of a Noble Person from the medical profession will ultimately guide you back to good health. You are advised to keep yourself healthy by participating in more physical activities, and keeping a healthy routine.

Monthly Luck

農曆正月 (February 4th - March 4th) 甲寅

Obstacles and impediments will affect your life and stunt your work progress. Your colleagues and superiors might begin to antagonise you and there could be an overwhelming amount of workload. To alleviate the situation, diligently concentrate on your social interactions at work and your job assignments.

農曆二月 (March 5th - April 4th) 乙卯

Similar to last month's outlook, this month could prove to be a hectic one. You will be continuously swamped by a seemingly insurmountable amount of work coupled with demanding and unappreciative superiors. Just like before, keep yourself consistently focused in all aspects of your job and make sensible judgments in your decision. These recommendations will help to minimize the mistakes you might make during this period.

農曆三月 (April 5th - May 4th) 丙辰

After the first two months of obstructions, favourable fortunes could start to appear in your life this month. Take advantage of this newfound revitalisation period to clear off all your pending tasks. During this time, you might also find that your superiors will be pleased with your satisfactory work performance. Invest in yourself by learning a new language or adopting a new sport in order to enhance your overall personality.

農曆四月 (May 5th - June 5th) 丁巳

Your luck will start to fluctuate this month, with both good and bad events transpiring in your life. Without you noticing, time will fly by quickly as your superiors start to make increasing demands from you. However, the generosity of good people around you will help to minimize the loss of time and burden of expectations that you could experience this month.

農曆五月 (June 6th - July 6th) 戊午

Those who are single can rejoice as this month brings you more opportunities in terms of love. Single Rooster individuals will be able to start a new relationship with someone they fancy. On the other hand, married individuals should not act on any passionate feelings they might have towards other individuals or else the relationship could swiftly fall apart.

農曆六月 (July 7th - August 6th) 己未

Undesirable situations at work could catch you off guard if you are not prepared, causing numerous mistakes to arise in your work performance. This constant preoccupation with your work will also keep you away from your family for longer periods of time, potentially weakening the bonds between you and your family members. It is essential that you schedule some time to hang out with your family to maintain a strong familial connection with them.

農曆七月 (August 7th - September 7th) 庚申

Legal issues stemming from personal disputes with your family or colleagues could arise this month. Refrain from assuming the role of a guarantor for other people or things may get more than a little dicey in the near future. Examine every single detail in a contract with the utmost diligence and attention before placing your signature on it to avoid any unpleasant repercussions later on.

農曆八月 (September 8th - October 7th) 辛酉

This month will shower you with numerous opportunities for you to display your talents and efforts front and centre. Do proceed carefully however as too much complacency on your part might see these golden chances go to waste. Additionally, expect your work performance to be significantly tested with your productivity taking a slight dip. Ensure that you perform your duties to standard and your work productivity will improve soon after.

農曆九月 (October 8th - November 6th) 壬戌

Be on guard for the many trials and tribulations that this month brings. Your spirit will be tested in both your personal and professional life. You can try to build upon new ideas that you have been concocting for the past few months. However, it would be relatively better if you would concentrate on the current workload to see out this month in a confident state. You should also pay attention to your words and actions when interacting with your work peers or you might get yourself into serious trouble.

農曆十月 (November 7th - December 6th) 癸亥

Similar to last month, this month's busy schedule will present more obstructions for you to deal with. Brace yourself for a busy period at work with your superiors scrutinising every detail. Diligence and resolve will be vital in order to navigate yourself out of these situations. In addition to that, let go of any loathing that you may have for your superiors' harsh behaviour and you will end the month with a positive attitude.

農曆十一月 (December 7th 2018 - January 4th 2019) 甲子

Your well-being should take centre stage among your priorities this month, with your body becoming more susceptible to various illnesses and dangers. Your immune system could suffer a heavy toll due to these afflictions if you are not on the alert. Thus, it best that you increase your intake of the necessary vitamins and minerals coupled with plenty of physical workouts to preserve your well-being.

農曆十二月 (January 5th - February 3rd 2019) 乙丑

The calendar year thankfully comes to a close on an optimistic note, with a great abundance of auspiciousness in all aspects of your life. Your career, finances and health will be in good shape. Moreover, you will successfully accomplish the goals that you have set out for yourself with bountiful rewards in return. Plus, you might receive a gift of extra wealth to cap off the year in a fruitful manner.

Personalised Forecast For 2018 Based on Day of Birth

(Assessment based on the 60 Jia Zi 甲子 Day Pillars)

甲子 Jia Zi Day

Overview

This is a rather moderate year for you, which can spell out a lack of excitement unless you make some effort to get things going. You may want to learn new ways of working and planning so that you gear up for some change and progress, especially if you are involved in the creative industry. Re-strategizing can help you revamp your outlook on work and help you achieve more exciting results.

Wealth

Long-term investments are a better bet than short-term ones this year as the latter are likely fall short and result in losses. Regardless, you should still exercise thorough analysis before making any decisions, especially when it comes to where you should be putting your money. Risks and gambles will do you no favours this year. You should think of the big picture and instead opt for saving.

Relationships

Single men may be lucky enough to find a significant other this year. However, single women are better off investing their time in other aspects of their lives such as work, which at least bears the potential to bring fruits. Married people may be troubled by the possibility of betrayal.

Health

You will enjoy overall good health, but you will still need to be careful while travelling as there is a chance for you to suffer from injuries to the head or feet. Those with a history of gastric problems may find the problem recurring this year. Despite these issues, your health outlook is generally positive, though you should still take some precautions.

Career

You are likely to have many career opportunities come your way this year. Be proactive about it and react with enthusiasm and forethought rather than wait for things to work out. Be sure to do preparatory work and carefully research your options. Diligence will ensure the best way forward for you.

農曆正月

(February 4th - March 4th) 甲寅
Stay alert on the road this month as there is a possibility of trouble such as vehicular accidents.

農曆二月

(March 5th - April 4th) 乙卯
You may find yourself rewarded at work this month that may come with great financial benefits.

農曆三月

(April 5th - May 4th) 丙辰
Be careful with your temper and do not let your emotions get too out of hand this month as this may lead to poor decisions and regrettable outcomes.

農曆四月

(May 5th - June 5th) 丁巳
Certain unfavourable circumstances may come in your way this month. Look out for trusted peers at work and in your personal life for support and solutions. Do not be afraid to confide in them and take their advice.

農曆五月

(June 6th - July 6th) 戊午
Exercise constant vigilance at work this month as there may be trouble brewing at your workplace with people out to turn the tide against you.

農曆六月

(July 7th - August 6th) 己未
You may experience some disagreements and discord with your significant other this month. This may also happen with your work associates. Try your best to keep a cool head and avoid as many arguments as possible.

農曆七月

(August 7th - September 7th) 庚申
Keep a firm hold of your emotions and do not let them get the better of you. Strong emotions such as envy may cause you to fall into negative circumstances. Be level headed and make reasonable decisions based on rationale.

農曆八月

(September 8th - October 7th) 辛酉
Travelling southward may do you some good this month. Firm decisions can lead to exciting actions for you as well.

農曆九月

(October 8th - November 6th) 壬戌
Look out for unscrupulous individuals at work who are trying to get the better of you using dirty tricks such as rumours. Ignore their devious efforts and instead focus on your own work.

農曆十月

(November 7th - December 6th) 癸亥
Do not shy away from working extra hard this month as that may be the only way you actually get to see results at work. Stand your ground and pull through. The effort will certainly pay off at the end of the day.

農曆十一月

(December 7th 2018 - January 4th 2019) 甲子
Be prudent when it comes to signing legal documents this month. Do not try to quickly get them out the way as this hastiness may lead to you unwillingly committing to terms that are not beneficial to you.

農曆十二月

(January 5th - February 3rd 2019) 乙丑
The focus should be on your health this month. Start the month well by getting a full body check-up where you can quickly detect potential issues and quickly seek the appropriate treatment. Be especially careful with your eyes and heart.

乙丑 **Yi Chou Day**

Overview

This will be a mellower year for you, especially in regards to your career. However, this does not mean it is time for you to take it easy either. Keep up your hard work and even try to use your spare time to learn new skills through various kinds of workshops or courses. This will not benefit your future career but also keep your current skills sharp and fine-tuned. Aside from this, you should refrain from pursuing fame or any kind of boost to your reputation this year.

 ## Wealth

Steer clear of short-term investments this year and opt for long-term investments instead. Utilize prudence and careful thinking on more solid options that are more likely to provide you with good returns, such as higher education or property. It is better to go for something that is more stable even though it may work slower, rather than something that provides only empty promises.

 ## Relationships

You will need to watch out for the unwanted advances of third parties encroaching into your relationship. One thing could lead to another so you should not take anything for granted. Be alert and always be sure of what is happening around you. This way, you can curb future problems by communicating with your partner instead of becoming suspicious later on.

 ## Health

You will need to take better care of your eyes and heart this year. This is a good time for you to rethink your health, diet and exercise routine. Gun for healthier dietary habits and remember to accompany your new diet with a proper fitness routine that will serve you well.

 ## Career

Your career will be smooth sailing for the most part this year. You will have the opportunity to pick up new skills which will help to boost your professional value. However, do not be too arrogant with your talents. Try to be more humble and introspective.

農曆正月

(February 4th - March 4th) 甲寅
You will have a good wealth outlook this month, though you will need to guard against overspending, especially if you were born in the autumn.

農曆二月

(March 5th - April 4th) 乙卯
Exercise discipline and focus in your work this month to reap rewards such as extra income.

農曆三月

(April 5th - May 4th) 丙辰
You will be more prone to overthinking and overanalysing.

農曆四月

(May 5th - June 5th) 丁巳
Competition heats up at the workplace this month. Be aware of the moves others are making, especially that of colleagues who may try to claim your ideas as their own.

農曆五月

(June 6th - July 6th) 戊午
Changes will come to the workplace this month in the form of a new superior. Do your best to make a good impression as you will want them in your network.

農曆六月

(July 7th - August 6th) 己未
You will have to put in extra hard on group projects and collaborations this month. Do not be afraid to spend more time working on new ideas and sharing them with your colleagues.

農曆七月

(August 7th - September 7th) 庚申
There is a chance that you may meet with some kind of accident this month, and as such you will need to be careful when you are on the road and be particularly careful with your right leg.

農曆八月

(September 8th - October 7th) 辛酉
You may find yourself prone to irritation and a quick temper this month. Learn how to calm yourself down and think rationally in order to avoid arguments.

農曆九月

(October 8th - November 6th) 壬戌
You will need to be prepared for changes to your work this month, both in terms of the style and pace. Your boss may throw something new at you that demands quick adaptation.

農曆十月

(November 7th - December 6th) 癸亥
This is not the right month to become involved in long-term investments. Your mind is not in the right place for such a heavy commitment.

農曆十一月

(December 7th 2018 - January 4th 2019) 甲子
Be careful while on the road this month, as breaking the law will result in a penalty.

農曆十二月

(January 5th - February 3rd 2019) 乙丑
Try not to let disappointment at work distract you from focusing, even if promises made by your boss were empty.

丙寅 Bing Yin Day

Overview

You can expect advancements in your professional and financial life. Work at winning the recognition of others at your workplace and gaining their endorsement. As such, it is crucial that you prove your capabilities and showcase your talents so others are fully aware what value you bring. Stay focused on your objectives and stick to a rigorous plan of action. Keep up your efforts and your dreams will eventually come true.

 ## Wealth

Your will have good luck when it comes to money and reputation this year, as you find yourself occupying the spotlight more often than not. This increased visibility will result in the broadening of your network with more contacts getting in touch to set up great opportunities for financial reward.

 ## Relationships

Single women will have high chances of finding a spouse this year. If you are in a long-term relationship, the time has come to settle down. If you are married, you may have to be on the alert for potential extramarital dalliances.

 ## Health

Even though you will enjoy good health this year, you should still maintain regular exercise, especially if you are over sixty years old. In general, there are some health issues that could crop up in terms of your digestive system so it is imperative that you go for a medical check-up as soon as you detect any symptoms.

 ## Career

Your work seems to be going smoothly this year and there will come many opportunities to advance in your career. You will have to determine what your goals are and be more aggressive in fighting for what you want.

農曆正月

(February 4th - March 4th) 甲寅
You will enjoy good wealth luck this month. You can make the most of it by being as efficient in your tasks as you can and seeking out new opportunities.

農曆二月

(March 5th - April 4th) 乙卯
You will find yourself getting pulled into many disagreements this month, due to financial problems. It will be important to stay rational when thinking about these problems.

農曆三月

(April 5th - May 4th) 丙辰
It will be crucial for you to separate your tasks at work with your other professional obligations this month or risk unnecessary misunderstandings.

農曆四月

(May 5th - June 5th) 丁巳
You should stay on the law's good side this month, as the tendency for legal trouble is rife.

農曆五月

(June 6th - July 6th) 戊午
You will need to execute your spending carefully and prudently this month, as there is a likelihood of sudden financial losses.

農曆六月

(July 7th - August 6th) 己未
There is a chance that your relationship or marriage will be tense this month, largely due to money problems.

農曆七月

(August 7th - September 7th) 庚申
There is a chance you will be gifted with a career advancement this month. This is also a positive month for single women, as you are likely to meet a prospective match.

農曆八月

(September 8th - October 7th) 辛酉
You will need to be careful while on the road this month, as there is a chance of breaking the law and incurring a penalty.

農曆九月

(October 8th - November 6th) 壬戌
Be careful with your words this month as they can have far-reaching effects, especially for women.

農曆十月

(November 7th - December 6th) 癸亥
You will be in dire need of a proper rest this month, and as such, make sure you take heed of your needs and respect them.

農曆十一月

(December 7th 2018 - January 4th 2019) 甲子
You will find yourself developing some great ideas this month, which can result in great work.

農曆十二月

(January 5th - February 3rd 2019) 乙丑
Your health should be the top of your priorities this month, especially your stomach. This is especially true if you were born in the winter.

丁卯 **Ding Mao Day**

Overview
You will find that this is an auspicious year bringing you opportunities and recognition as your hard work finally pays off and brings you great results. Your bosses are happy with your performance and reward you with promotions or career advancements. There is much to look forward to in the future so do keep up your efforts.

 Wealth

You will come into your place as a recognised and respected individual at your workplace. While your financial outlook seems rather lukewarm, this increase in reputation enables you to set up a strong foundation for future wealth pursuits. It will also help you establish important networks that will benefit you financially in the future.

 Relationships

Single women need to be more proactive in pursuing a significant other this year as being too passive will not yield any results. Men are likely to encounter romantic opportunities in the first, second, eleventh and twelfth months. Be open with your options and you may just find the right person for you. Do not shy away from making the first move.

 Health

Your upper torso in particular is at risk this year of injury. Immediately seek out a doctor if you begin to feel unwell so you curb any problems from worsening. Be mindful of bone-related injuries as well as these issues can be quite serious.

 Career

Your career prospects are in an upswing this year, especially if you were born in the spring or winter months. Your hard work will not go unnoticed for long and as such you need to keep up your efforts.

農曆正月

(February 4th - March 4th) 甲寅
You will enjoy good Financial Luck this month and possibly even be blessed with some unexpected financial rewards.

農曆二月

(March 5th - April 4th) 乙卯
Your wealth luck continues to flourish this month. This may be a good time for you to ask for a pay raise at work.

農曆三月

(April 5th - May 4th) 丙辰
You continue to experience good luck, especially with your career this month. This means a possible promotion or career advancement.

農曆四月

(May 5th - June 5th) 丁巳
Single women will enjoy positive romance luck this month. Do not be afraid to step out and make the first move.

農曆五月

(June 6th - July 6th) 戊午
Your domestic life may be quite stormy as there are many disagreements to deal with in which you will need to exercise patience and misunderstandings.

農曆六月

(July 7th - August 6th) 己未
Do not let your impulsive instincts override your reason in terms of your spending this month. Be disciplined with how you use your money.

農曆七月

(August 7th - September 7th) 庚申
This is a good month for travelling. Do not be afraid to pursue long-held fantasies of seeing the world.

農曆八月

(September 8th - October 7th) 辛酉
Your social life will experience a boom this month. Your network will grow larger and you will be swept up in parties and gatherings. However, you should refrain overindulging in alcohol.

農曆九月

(October 8th - November 6th) 壬戌
Those born in the summer may find themselves battling stress this month, whereas those born in the spring will enjoy good luck in showcasing their talents and earning recognition.

農曆十月

(November 7th - December 6th) 癸亥
Your creativity is at its full potential this month, leading to brand new ideas in dealing with old projects. You will thus be able to revamp these old prospects.

農曆十一月

(December 7th 2018 - January 4th 2019) 甲子
Good business prospects will come your way leading to profitable results. As such, you should start planning now so that you are prepared for the changes to come.

農曆十二月

(January 5th - February 3rd 2019) 乙丑
This is a good month for you to think about investments as your financial luck is looking good.

戊辰 **Wu Chen Day**

Overview
You will experience a good year full of promising outcomes. Those born in the spring will certainly find this to be a beneficial time. Short-term investments will bear fruit while business ventures also experience excellent prospects. Long-term investments will be encouraged by your diligence and will eventually yield great results.

 ## Wealth
Your wealth luck is in upswing this year and you will reap significant rewards. That being said, you should still spend wisely so as to not squander what you have just made. Avoid impulse purchases and try to reinvest your money on other activities that bring more benefit to you.

 ## Relationships
This year, married men will enjoy many improvements in their marriage. On the other hand, women will have to deal with communication issues in their relationship that could lead to misunderstandings and arguments.

Health
Focus on your digestive system this year as stomach problems are likely to be your biggest health concern this year. Your head and limbs are also at potential risk of injury, especially for those born during the summer or autumn.

Career
You are likely to receive critical acclaim for the great effort you have put into your work thus far. Both your superiors and peers will accordingly praise you for your progress. That being said, your talents will be a reason for your superiors to push more of the workload onto your shoulders. Their expectations will have surged and as such you will need to be prepared for the potential chaos and stress of the coming year. Remember to balance your work with time for yourself and your personal life.

農曆正月

(February 4th - March 4th) 甲寅
This will be a busy month as you have a lot on your plate. Do take some time off to recalibrate and rest so that you keep things in perspective. This helps you to stay alert to the potential backstabbing that jealous individuals at work may be planning against you.

農曆二月

(March 5th - April 4th) 乙卯
You will be graced with the support and encouragement of many people in your life. Work with them and you will find that your goals are easier met with the help.

農曆三月

(April 5th - May 4th) 丙辰
Your Financial Luck is positive this month. As such, you should seek out opportunities to generate more wealth and see how these plans can help you make some extra income. Do not be too idle as you will miss out on these opportunities.

農曆四月

(May 5th - June 5th) 丁巳
Prospects and ideas from the past may resurface, this time in better conditions. You will be able to make something of these opportunities so that they result in positive outcomes.

農曆五月

(June 6th - July 6th) 戊午
Take some time off this month to relax. This month will be filled with stressful emotions and increased workloads, so do not be afraid to step out of the scene for a while to collect yourself. There is also a likelihood of a head injury and as such you should be accordingly cautious.

農曆六月

(July 7th - August 6th) 己未
Persons over the age of forty may have to go through a minor surgery this month. Do not be alarmed as your concerns can be easily softened if you take the time to discuss things with your doctor.

農曆七月

(August 7th - September 7th) 庚申
This is a time for action. It will not do you any good to sit and plan for too long without any actual progress. Waiting too long may result in you losing out on opportunities.

農曆八月

(September 8th - October 7th) 辛酉
There is a chance you may receive bonuses or benefits at work. However, you will need to speak up for yourself and ask for these perks. If not, these opportunities will pass you by.

農曆九月

(October 8th - November 6th) 壬戌
Competition heats up at the workplace this month, causing you to stress out over the energy and time you have to invest. Also, do take care of your spending so that you do not go into debt.

農曆十月

(November 7th - December 6th) 癸亥
Keep your priorities straight so that you do not lose focus and let others overtake your position. Make sure you do not lose momentum and keep working hard.

農曆十一月

(December 7th 2018 - January 4th 2019) 甲子
You may have to adapt to sudden changes in your plans this month. Be open to the possible changes as they might actually serve to improve your situation.

農曆十二月

(January 5th - February 3rd 2019) 乙丑
It is time for you to drop your emotional baggage and move forward with your life. The new year should begin with a fresh start, without the weight of the past holding you down.

己巳 Ji Si Day

Overview

Your prospects for wealth are excellent this year. You will need to focus on expanding your social network and how to properly take advantage of it in order to seize the opportunities available to you. However, you are likely to be plagued by gossip and false accusations, especially if you were born in the autumn. It is best to ignore these rumours and focus on your goals.

 ## Wealth

Most of your opportunities will arise from your social circles this year. By being more sociable and strategic, you can strengthen your professional reputation and also gain prestige. While you may be able to make quite a bit of money, you should still exercise caution and prudence when it comes to investments and opt for more stable options such as property.

 ## Relationships

If you are a man, you will have auspicious Peach Blossom Luck this year which carries with it the possibility of marriage. However, women will not be so lucky. If things do not turn out the way you hoped, concentrate instead on other areas of your life as things will ultimately work out for you.

 ## Health

This year, you will need to be more mindful of your heart and eyes. Fever may also be a frequent problem this year so you will have to take good care of yourself in order to prevent yourself from falling ill. Furthermore, your energy levels are easily depleted this year.

 ## Career

Work-related trips will be your ticket to career advancement this year. This includes out-of-town assignments. However, you may feel used by your superiors and could find yourself suffocating from your many burdens at work, causing frustration and dissatisfaction. Remember that your current situation is only temporary and that the rewards are long term.

農曆正月

(February 4th - March 4th) 甲寅
Good news will come your way this month, especially if you were born during the autumn or winter, even the chance for some wealth.

農曆二月

(March 5th - April 4th) 乙卯
Travel brings the possibility of wealth this month, so pack up and go on an adventure. You will need to remember avoid stress and work during your downtime so that you can fully relax.

農曆三月

(April 5th - May 4th) 丙辰
There is a possibility of a new job offer this month. You should consider your options thoroughly before deciding as this could possibly be the change you need in your life right now.

農曆四月

(May 5th - June 5th) 丁巳
You will need to work extra hard to retain focus and concentration this month. Discipline is needed, especially for those born in the winter.

農曆五月

(June 6th - July 6th) 戊午
You will be full of ideas this month, but you will need to frame and organise them well, in order to make the best of them.

農曆六月

(July 7th - August 6th) 己未
The grass always seems greener on the other side. Do not waste your time envying others and instead be grateful for what you have.

農曆七月

(August 7th - September 7th) 庚申
There is a risk of health troubles this year if you do not watch your diet, especially in terms of food poisoning or stomach flu.

農曆八月

(September 8th - October 7th) 辛酉
Heart-related issues may crop up this month, especially if you are older. It will be best to be prepared and ready to quickly take the proper measures to avoid the worst of it.

農曆九月

(October 8th - November 6th) 壬戌
If you own a business or supervise anyone, there is the likelihood of problems with your staff that you will need to watch out for, including household staff.

農曆十月

(November 7th - December 6th) 癸亥
You will be irritable throughout the mouth and prone to being careless with words, so try to keep your temper in check to avoid offending your colleagues.

農曆十一月

(December 7th 2018 - January 4th 2019) 甲子
Travelling south will bring great benefits to you this month. You should also try to avoid working alone as teamwork will greatly improve your chances with wealth.

農曆十二月

(January 5th - February 3rd 2019) 乙丑
This is the month for you to pull back and spend more time with your family, as it is possible that they have been feeling neglected.

庚午 Geng Wu Day

Overview

Your year ahead is looking more positive as your efforts over the years begin to pay off, particularly if you are professional or consider yourself a white-collar worker. Keep up your efforts in order to continue building your foundation and solidifying your reputation.

 ### Wealth

You need to understand how important pro-activeness is when it comes to financial matters. Let loose your adventurous side and pursue endeavours that you might never have thought about before. Try out new approaches and get creative with your methods to yield interesting results.

 ### Relationships

If you are in a long-term relationship or are married, you may experience quite a bit of emotional turmoil. You will need to be very patient in dealing with this so that you do not lose your temper and cause a bigger rift. Choose your battles wisely and opt for compromise.

 ### Health

You may likely be plagued by blood-related illnesses and skin allergies. As such, you will need to get regular medical check-ups and maintain a healthy diet, being wary of stomach and food poisoning issues as well. If ignored, these issues could develop into chronic problems. Rethink your dietary habits and make changes accordingly.

 ### Career

You may start to think about changing jobs or positions. Travel is also a possibility, especially if it is work related. Be more flexible and open-minded during these endeavours. If you own a business, you must be more alert than usual as there may be problems within your organisation that you will have to curb early on.

農曆正月

(February 4th - March 4th) 甲寅
Those who own their own businesses will find that this is a difficult and competitive month. There is a chance they may lose some of their valuable staff.

農曆二月

(March 5th - April 4th) 乙卯
Strong competition continues on this month, especially for those born in the summer. Re-evaluate your plans and think of new ways to combat your competitors.

農曆三月

(April 5th - May 4th) 丙辰
Steer clear of hasty decisions this month and instead adopt the habit of thinking carefully to avoid future regrets.

農曆四月

(May 5th - June 5th) 丁巳
Try to ignore potential stress this month or you risk getting too affected and succumbing to stress-related skin problems, such as rashes or other allergies. Learn how to let go every once in a while.

農曆五月

(June 6th - July 6th) 戊午
You will experience positive Wealth Luck this month especially if you were born in the winter. Use this to your advantage – for instance, if you feel a pay raise is long overdue, now is the time to ask for one.

農曆六月

(July 7th - August 6th) 己未
Your auspicious Wealth Luck continues on this month and as such, you should take this opportunity to think of new ideas to implement.

農曆七月

(August 7th - September 7th) 庚申
Steer clear of rule breaking or unethical shortcuts this month as it will only lead to future legal troubles.

農曆八月

(September 8th - October 7th) 辛酉
Those who were born in the autumn or winter will benefit greatly from working in close collaboration with others this month.

農曆九月

(October 8th - November 6th) 壬戌
Arguments may crop up this month between you and your significant other, with jealousy and insecurity being the most serious motivating factors.

農曆十月

(November 7th - December 6th) 癸亥
Your emotions are chaotic this month, making it difficult for you to stay focused. Seek unbiased perspectives from others so that you can recalibrate your thoughts and make better decisions.

農曆十一月

(December 7th 2018 - January 4th 2019) 甲子
This is a good month for becoming involved in partnerships and joint ventures. Take up the opportunity should it present itself.

農曆十二月

(January 5th - February 3rd 2019) 乙丑
You will find yourself rather stressed this month, though you should not let it get to you. You can step back every once in a while to recover your mind.

辛未 **Xin Wei Day**

Xin

Wei

Overview

This will be a fast and busy year for you especially if you are a full-time employee or if you were born in the summer. You may have to adhere to a stringent, task-oriented schedule and may possible even be assigned to a foreign country. This can be discouraging for you, but you should instead use this as an opportunity for self-discovery.

 Wealth

You may feel tempted to spend money on frivolous and luxurious things. However, remember that material possessions only last so long and will dwindle your resources. If you successfully control your spending, your wealth opportunities will improve towards the end of the year.

 Relationships

This year is likely to be emotionally turbulent and tumultuous for couples. You will need to frankly assess if you are willing to be in this relationship for the long haul. If so, you must take the necessary steps and work hard to mend your relationship. Control your emotions and work to compromise.

 Health

Be on watch for your cholesterol level by going for frequent medical inspections, especially if you are thirty or older. Potential food and skin allergies might also plague you. Be sure to balance your work and leisure time so you do not get too stressed to the point where your health is affected.

 Career

Be ready to tackle a series of challenges and obstacles in your career. Work hard at pushing on so that you will eventually overcome your troubles and triumph in the rewards you deserve. Take this as an opportunity to prove yourself.

農曆正月

(February 4th - March 4th) 甲寅
Engage in teamwork with others as it will help you reach your goals faster and more effectively this month.

農曆二月

(March 5th - April 4th) 乙卯
Networking will help you gain valuable contacts and assistance in your goals and tasks at work this month. Through this, there will be a possibility of garnering assistance from Noble People.

農曆三月

(April 5th - May 4th) 丙辰
Do not fall prey to procrastination and turn to improvised plans for solutions. You will need to be prepared and have good contingencies.

農曆四月

(May 5th - June 5th) 丁巳
Exercise more discipline with your spending this month, as there is a risk of financial woes.

農曆五月

(June 6th - July 6th) 戊午
Those who were born in the summer will experience strong feelings of envy. Work hard to mitigate this feeling and think more positively so that you are not distracted from your work.

農曆六月

(July 7th - August 6th) 己未
You may be blessed with a great idea this month that can benefit you greatly to the point that it can finance your travels.

農曆七月

(August 7th - September 7th) 庚申
You may advance in your career through either a promotion or salary increase this month, especially if you are a full-time worker.

農曆八月

(September 8th - October 7th) 辛酉
Do not let yourself be coerced by your peers into breaking the law this month regardless of how much you crave their approval.

農曆九月

(October 8th - November 6th) 壬戌
You will begin to feel as if you have been taken for granted this month. However, this idea does not have its roots in reality, and as such, you should nip it in the bud.

農曆十月

(November 7th - December 6th) 癸亥
You will have good Wealth Luck this month and will have the opportunity to make more money, especially if you were born in the autumn.

農曆十一月

(December 7th 2018 - January 4th 2019) 甲子
Be extra cautious about your food allergies this month, as it may lead to serious health issues. In general, try to pay more attention to your well-being.

農曆十二月

(January 5th - February 3rd 2019) 乙丑
Your partner may be exuding antagonistic behaviour this month, but you should avoid arguments as much as possible.

壬申 Ren Shen Day

Ren

Shen

Overview

This is a year of unexpected benefits. Instead of financial gain, the focus will be more on your social and professional network. Through these avenues, you can scout for new opportunities that would have otherwise been inaccessible. However, the year may prove to be socially exhaustive. Bear in mind that you do not need to entertain every single social opportunity. Just stay true to yourself and remember that it is okay to take some time off every now and then.

 Wealth

While you may value your independence, your tasks will be easier dealt with if you engage the assistance of a group of people. This is especially true for those born in the autumn or winter. Investments could be problematic, though not entirely off the books. Consider the investments that are more long term and low-risk.

 Relationships

Couples will greatly improve in their intimacy, bonding and trust. However, petty arguments have the potential of turning into something more serious if neither party can effectively compromise. Be patient with one another and prioritise honest communication.

 Health

Those above the age of forty need to take more care of their sugar intake. Also be mindful of your stomach as there is possibility of complications. Watch out for what kind of food you consume so as to not cause any unnecessary problems.

 Career

Travel will help expand your horizons and give you new avenues and ideas. You will be reinvigorated by your experiences. You may also change jobs, and as such you will need to keep your options open and think about what the best move is for you. Do not be afraid to step out of your comfort zone.

農曆正月

(February 4th - March 4th) 甲寅
Those born in the summer will struggle at work with impressing their superiors. They may find that the bosses favour their colleagues over them.

農曆二月

(March 5th - April 4th) 乙卯
You may receive a good offer to change your career this month. This offer will provide you with new wealth opportunities. Do take some time to weigh your options carefully before deciding.

農曆三月

(April 5th - May 4th) 丙辰
You will have to contend with conflicts on two fronts, both at home and at work. Be patient with and stay calm even in the face of bombardments. Do not let small disagreements devolve into senseless arguments.

農曆四月

(May 5th - June 5th) 丁巳
Your workplace stress will greatly increase this month. If an opportunity to travel north for work presents itself, grab the opportunity as it will result in great benefits.

農曆五月

(June 6th - July 6th) 戊午
You may be given a new project this that you should invest your best efforts into. Successful completion of this project may open up new avenues for you to progress in your career.

農曆六月

(July 7th - August 6th) 己未
Be mindful of a potentially volatile temper this month. Be careful with your words as you are prone to offending or hurting others. Do not let this happen as it will lead to irreparable fractures in your relationships.

農曆七月

(August 7th - September 7th) 庚申
Your wealth prospects are looking up this month and as such, do not let your situation devolve again by being careless with what you have.

農曆八月

(September 8th - October 7th) 辛酉
Do not let your pride get in the way of accepting and working with other peoples' opinions and criticisms. Be open to the idea that they may be trying to help you, especially with your finances.

農曆九月

(October 8th - November 6th) 壬戌
You may have to grapple with stress at work. Make sure you take some time for yourself to keep your cool and relax every now and then.

農曆十月

(November 7th - December 6th) 癸亥
Be mindful of the condition of your stomach this month as there is possible of ailments. This is especially the case for those travelling north. Take caution in what you eat and also with hygiene.

農曆十一月

(December 7th 2018 - January 4th 2019) 甲子
A number of close friends will approach you offering advice regarding your relationship issues. You can take into stock their advice but do exercise some scrutiny.

農曆十二月

(January 5th - February 3rd 2019) 乙丑
Every successful marriage requires both sides to be communicative and trusting of one another. Married people should bear this in mind during arguments and bouts of suspicion as this will cause problems for your relationship.

癸酉 Gui You Day

Gui

You

Overview

The year ahead will be a challenging one for you. However, there is potential solution. Your obstacles can be dealt if you undertake some contingency planning to hold out for the worst. The silver lining is that you will certainly learn from the hardships of this year. If there are existing conflicts between you and your superior, those issue may escalate this year. Nevertheless, be patient and hold out, as it is not the right time to switch jobs.

 Wealth

You are not in the position to be making hasty decisions on risky investments. Speculative or short-term investments will not bring you any benefit. Work at maintaining your current wealth by saving and spending wisely.

 Relationships

Married couples will need to stay strong to pull through the year. Be faithful in your commitment to work on your marriage. Single people will be better off not getting involved in romance this year, as it is not an auspicious time for such matters.

 Health

Other than the inevitable stress and pressure as a result of other aspects of your life, your physical health is rather good. Mental and emotional turbulence will trouble you, but you can practice some calming physical activities to help mitigate the negative effects. Do keep going for medical check-ups just in case.

 Career

The main problem for you at work is a lack of recognition and appreciation. However, do not let the frustration force you into a change of career, as the outcome is likely unfavourable. Stay focused at your current job so that you do not compromise your position even more.

農曆正月

(February 4th - March 4th) 甲寅
You will face some problems at work this month as you begin to suspect that your superiors do not appreciate your work.

農曆二月

(March 5th - April 4th) 乙卯
People born in the summer will be more affected than other by the misfortune of this month. Try to be less stubborn and you will find that your situation improves.

農曆三月

(April 5th - May 4th) 丙辰
Inspiration will elude you this month. Do not be bogged down by frustration; instead, stay focused and power through your work to avoid a backlog of burdens later.

農曆四月

(May 5th - June 5th) 丁巳
This continues to be a stagnant month without much progress. You will find yourself being rather inactive. Try being more introspective and think about how you can improve.

農曆五月

(June 6th - July 6th) 戊午
Those working in an artistic or creative field will find that this is a more productive month. Inspiration will come easier and you will produce better and more work.

農曆六月

(July 7th - August 6th) 己未
You should take a break this month, though remain vigilant about your physical health, as there is a chance of injury on your right leg.

農曆七月

(August 7th - September 7th) 庚申
Your Wealth Luck will improve this month, though you should not get overexcited and ruin your prospects by making the wrong decisions.

農曆八月

(September 8th - October 7th) 辛酉
This month proves to be challenging particularly in terms of your emotional state. You will find yourself hampered by mood swings which will make it difficult to focus on work.

農曆九月

(October 8th - November 6th) 壬戌
You may start feeling taken for granted this month, like others are taking advantage of you. Do not be afraid to stand up for yourself and demand what you are owed.

農曆十月

(November 7th - December 6th) 癸亥
Those born in the winter should avoid water-based activities this month as there is a possibility of injuries.

農曆十一月

(December 7th 2018 - January 4th 2019) 甲子
Try not to spend too much time shopping for trivial products this month as there is a possibility of overspending. Be mindful of your budget and work at saving your money.

農曆十二月

(January 5th - February 3rd 2019) 乙丑
Do not hesitate to share some of your ideas with your friends this month. You will find that they make valuable earpieces.

甲戌 Jia Xu Day

Overview

Your Dog year will sail along smoothly for much of the time. There will be few sudden changes to shock you along the way. This also means that positive changes are also rather slow. For instance, there is a low chance of receiving praise or advancement at work. However, you should not give up. Keep working hard as this lays the foundation for future endeavours.

 ## Wealth

Progress with your wealth may be rather disappointing this year. However, this does not mean that you should slow down and let the momentum die out. Your efforts now will help you bear fruits in the future.

 ## Relationships

Your luck with romance is similarly mediocre. However, this means that you will have more free time to pursue other endeavours in your life. Those already in a relationship that does not seem to be very rewarding to either party should try to spend more time together and hopefully ignite the lost spark.

 ## Health

You will experience good health in general this year. That being said, there may be some minor issues with your eyes. Do get yourself treated early on. In addition, your limbs are also injury prone. As such, you will need to take extra care when performing strenuous activities.

 ## Career

This will not be a good year for you to be making changes in your career. Hold out at your current job and keep up the good work so that you will receive rewards for your perseverance later.

農曆正月

(February 4th - March 4th) 甲寅
Your Financial Luck is rather favourable this year, especially if you born in the winter. If you will be embarking on travels, do make sure you watch your budget as there is a risk of overspending.

農曆二月

(March 5th - April 4th) 乙卯
Your Wealth Luck is similarly positive this month, though you should not this for granted by slacking off. Try to be proactive so that you keep the momentum going.

農曆三月

(April 5th - May 4th) 丙辰
Remember to remain hard at work despite already achieving your goals. There is no good reason to let laziness take over as this will mean lack of practice and experience later when you have to get back on your feet.

農曆四月

(May 5th - June 5th) 丁巳
You may find yourself the victim of malicious gossip spread by others who are jealous of your success and relative stability. Try to ignore the drama as much as possible to just focus on your own well-being.

農曆五月

(June 6th - July 6th) 戊午
Competition at the workplace is surging, causing you to improve your efforts and work harder. Stay focused and you will come out on top.

農曆六月

(July 7th - August 6th) 己未
We are our own biggest doubters. Have faith in yourself that you can pull through and achieve your goals. Combat hesitation with confidence and determination.

農曆七月

(August 7th - September 7th) 庚申
You may be experience much confusion in your life at this point, causing you to stall on important decisions and dragging problems out.

農曆八月

(September 8th - October 7th) 辛酉
You may be hit by a bout of moodswings resulting in aggressive, explosive emotions. Do your best to control your emotions especially in the middle of conflicts, so as to not worsen the situation.

農曆九月

(October 8th - November 6th) 壬戌
Men in relationships, including married men, will have to face many temptations outside of their relationships this month. Keep your good sense and make sure not to betray the trust and love of your significant other.

農曆十月

(November 7th - December 6th) 癸亥
This is a good month for you to embark on travels. Travelling for work is a good way to get started. This will reap financial rewards for you and in addition, you can gain new experiences.

農曆十一月

(December 7th 2018 - January 4th 2019) 甲子
Make sure you read through any official documents or paperwork carefully before committing your signature in order to avoid legal troubles. Avoid peers who are a negative influence.

農曆十二月

(January 5th - February 3rd 2019) 乙丑
Your superiors may be trying to interfere with your work, causing you stress and dissatisfaction. The only solution is to communicate properly with them and make sure the discussion is diplomatic and mature.

乙亥 **Yi Hai Day**

Overview

Those born in the autumn and winter will experience a more positive year ahead. Meanwhile, those born in the spring and summer will have to exercise more caution around their peers as there is a risk of you being vulnerable to potential backstabbing or rumours. You are not obligated to always be of service to others lest they exploit your kindness. Take this time to truly discern who is worth your friendship.

 ## Wealth

Those born during the winter will experience positive wealth luck. There will be many offers coming your way to work with individuals who appreciate your hard work and talent. However, there will be immense competition heading your way. You will need to be more aggressive to ensure that others do not try to rob you of your position.

 ## Relationships

Those who are already married or in relationships will have to grapple with their partners experiencing insecurity and suspicion. Do not be too dismissive of their worries as this will show your insensitivity and impatience. Instead, try to discover the root problem and address the issue accordingly so that you put this matter at rest for the long run.

 ## Health

If you are born in the autumn, you will need to take better care of your stomach and digestive system. Everyone else may experience headaches and migraines that come as a result of poor stress management. Make sure you care for your emotional and mental health as much as your physical health.

 ## Career

Your creative nature and desire to innovate will impress your superiors. However, this may draw unwanted scrutiny from your colleagues. Be mindful of potential actions they may be trying to take against you so that you guard against others trying to uproot everything you worked hard to put into place. Do not let others tread over you and stand up for yourself.

農曆正月

(February 4th - March 4th) 甲寅
You will finally be able to cash in on favours from your colleague and your extended work networks to great rewards.

農曆二月

(March 5th - April 4th) 乙卯
There may be changes coming at work in the form of a new superior. Make sure you make a good first impression so that you start off on the right foot.

農曆三月

(April 5th - May 4th) 丙辰
Do not be easily swayed by temptations that come your way this month, even though the short-term benefits seem worth it.

農曆四月

(May 5th - June 5th) 丁巳
Look out for the possibility of malicious individuals around you looking to backstab and spread rumours about you. Make sure you discern carefully who to trust. Avoid these people as best you can and enjoy a drama-free month.

農曆五月

(June 6th - July 6th) 戊午
You will be fortunate enough to receive assistance from others this month, especially if you were born during the spring. Do not shy away from this and instead make the most of it.

農曆六月

(July 7th - August 6th) 己未
You will experience more stress at the workplace this month as opponents step up and try to pry away your hard earned rewards. Be firm in return so that you show your bosses you have a strong character.

農曆七月

(August 7th - September 7th) 庚申
Women in particular may find themselves plagued by relationship issues this month where they feel like they are being taken advantage of or underestimated.

農曆八月

(September 8th - October 7th) 辛酉
You may find yourself overwhelmed by a surge of expenses this month. Do not let the stress get to you wherein you begin to develop a drinking habit. As long as you watch out for your spending, you will be able to pull through.

農曆九月

(October 8th - November 6th) 壬戌
Try to be more spontaneous with your decision making so as to not waste time. This will also help you to trust your instincts more. As long as you are alert, you should be able to make the right decisions.

農曆十月

(November 7th - December 6th) 癸亥
Those born in the spring or winter will have to face several health problems this month. As such, pay more attention to your health so that you mitigate the worst effects.

農曆十一月

(December 7th 2018 - January 4th 2019) 甲子
You will experience highs and lows in quick succession as you go through a roller coaster ride of emotions. Try to exercise more control so that you keep things in perspective. If you are travelling, try to head south.

農曆十二月

(January 5th - February 3rd 2019) 乙丑
Women may have to deal with a third party who is trying to interfere in their relationship. Stay alert as this third party may be planning something behind your back.

丙子 Bing Zi Day

Overview

This year will prove to be rather challenging and busy for you. Careful that you do not get overwhelmed to the point of breaking down. While staying on track to complete your goals, you need to remember that you are allowed to take things easy every once in a while. Perhaps try focusing on one task at a time. Do not hesitate to take some time off for yourself to rejuvenate.

 ## Wealth

There is a possibility of financial losses this year. Be mindful of your budget so that you do not overspend and bring yourself irreversible financial damage. You will enjoy better luck in the first half of the year, but towards the middle of the year you will need to start tightening your expenditures.

 ## Relationships

If you are a woman in a relationship, there is a possibility of settling down with your significant other this year for good. However, married women may find this to be a difficult time that brings stress and emotional turmoil. Try to resolve disagreements diplomatically so that you do not let things go out of control. Men on the other hand should try to stay faithful to their relationship so that they do not neglect it for other temporary rewards.

 ## Health

Some minor health issues may crop up this year, especially towards the second half of the year. Those born in autumn and winter should be particularly mindful of this. Try to better your diet so that it is healthier and participate in some regular exercise. You will also need to mindful of your personal safety, particular when it comes to water activities.

 ## Career

You may find yourself disagreeing with your superiors at work this year. Make sure you learn how to mediate arguments carefully so that you do not jeopardize your bosses' impression of you. Hone your communication skills and establish strong bonds with your subordinates, so that you have support at work.

農曆正月

(February 4th - March 4th) 甲寅

Your year will get off to a good start with a month that brings you good wealth luck. Opportunities will come find you and you may even get promoted at work.

農曆二月

(March 5th - April 4th) 乙卯

This is the right month for you to capitalize on opportunities so that you may reap some significant financial rewards.

農曆三月

(April 5th - May 4th) 丙辰

Try to innovate so that you do not get bogged down with boredom. Step out of your comfort zone to explore new things, but be reasonable regarding your limits.

農曆四月

(May 5th - June 5th) 丁巳

Now is not the time for you to procrastinate or jump into action without proper planning. Stay alert and focused on your tasks.

農曆五月

(June 6th - July 6th) 戊午

Do not jump the gun on decisions. Too much spontaneity will only bring trouble to you and as such you will need to be more prudent.

農曆六月

(July 7th - August 6th) 己未

There may be an opportunity for you to embark on some travelling for work this month. This will bring you more wealth opportunities and an increase in reputation.

農曆七月

(August 7th - September 7th) 庚申

You may be experiencing some stressful health problems this month, particular concerning your stomach.

農曆八月

(September 8th - October 7th) 辛酉

There is a chance that some short-term investment schemes out there could do you some good and bring financial rewards.

農曆九月

(October 8th - November 6th) 壬戌

Your Wealth Luck experiences a surge in positivity this month as previous financial endeavours begin to bear fruit.

農曆十月

(November 7th - December 6th) 癸亥

There may be increased competition at work for you this month. If you are in a partnership, keep an eye on your partner to make sure they are doing their part.

農曆十一月

(December 7th 2018 - January 4th 2019) 甲子

Married couples will experience some difficulty this month, as old arguments resurface and tensions surge on the home front.

農曆十二月

(January 5th - February 3rd 2019) 乙丑

You will have the opportunity to embark on new financial endeavours this month. Stay focused and work hard so that you make the most of your time.

丁丑 Ding Chou Day

Overview

This is an auspicious year for those who were born during spring. Your financial outlook is solid and you will have many opportunities to widen your knowledge base and gain a renewed outlook on the world around you. Further education is in the books for you, as you will find yourself greatly empowered by the intellectual stimulation and growth you gain as a result.

 ## Wealth

You may start the year feeling as if your finances are not meeting your expectations. Fret not, your situation will certainly improve as you apply yourself in more creative ways and seek more unorthodox methods of accumulating wealth. Strategic and careful thinking can help you make the most of your situation and come out on top with significant growth.

 ## Relationships

Single women can experience better love luck this year with a good number of romantic opportunities awaiting you. That being said, you will need to get out there and mingle in order for these opportunities to be available for you. Single men may find themselves being led to a partner through their mothers' recommendations.

 ## Health

Look out for health problems related to your kidneys and bladder this year. Take note that this is due to unhealthy eating habits. As such, you need to perhaps go on a diet or remove some unhealthy foods from your daily routine. Rethinking your dietary habits may greatly change your health outlook for the better.

 ## Career

You will need to embrace all the learning opportunities that come your way this year through your work. This attitude will open up many more opportunities for you. Your superiors may suggest for you to pursue training or further studies, which is an excellent chance for you to improve yourself and earn an edge against others.

農曆正月

(February 4th - March 4th) 甲寅
You will have many opportunities to increase your finances this month. Stay alert for them and be ready to act when they arrive.

農曆二月

(March 5th - April 4th) 乙卯
This will be a month of trials and fatigue for married men as your spouse may be demanding more attention and care from you, taking you away from your work.

農曆三月

(April 5th - May 4th) 丙辰
Determination and strategy are needed in order for you to progress with your work this month. Stay out of unnecessary conflicts and focus on your work at hand.

農曆四月

(May 5th - June 5th) 丁巳
This is not a good month for you to partake in the signage of any legal documents, especially those related to property or land. Put it off to next month for better results and more auspicious conditions.

農曆五月

(June 6th - July 6th) 戊午
Many opportunities for wealth will come your way this month. Be ready for them and seize the opportunities when they are presented to you.

農曆六月

(July 7th - August 6th) 己未
Those born during the autumn or winter may find themselves bogged down by confusion and uncertainty this month. Seek clarity and balance so that you can start recalibrating your thoughts and perceptions.

農曆七月

(August 7th - September 7th) 庚申
Devious opponents are out to get you this month, trying to throw you off and gain an upper hand. Ignore their antics and thus render their efforts fruitless.

農曆八月

(September 8th - October 7th) 辛酉
Familial problems are at the forefront of your troubles this month, especially problems related to your mother. Try to be understanding instead of confrontational so that you can talk instead of fight.

農曆九月

(October 8th - November 6th) 壬戌
A new assignment or project may come your way at work this month. Take advantage of this new opportunity to prove yourself and showcase your worth.

農曆十月

(November 7th - December 6th) 癸亥
Those born during the autumn or winter are poised to travel southward this month.

農曆十一月

(December 7th 2018 - January 4th 2019) 甲子
Your opponents may start coming out in stronger forces this month, but do not let them distract you from your goals.

農曆十二月

(January 5th - February 3rd 2019) 乙丑
You will receive a small but welcome income from side projects that you have had to work hard on. The rewards of your diligence will have been worth it.

戊寅 **Wu Yin Day**

Overview

There will be a good number of workable opportunities gracing your career this year, possibly in the form of a promotion or travel opportunity for business. It will be good to actively pursue these leads and make something of them. However, there will be no shortage of confusion and ambiguity in your personal life this year, and similarly, you will need to be proactive in your pursuit to have these questions answered.

Wealth

You will finally have the means to bring your long awaited vacation and travelling plans to fruition. Form these travel opportunities, you will have the chance to broaden your horizons and meet new people who can help you along the path of personal growth. This is a good year for you to learn more about yourself and make improvements.

Relationships

This may be an auspicious year for romance for those you are already in long-term relationships or who are planning to take things to the next level. It will be helpful for the two of you to have a proper discussion about your plans and be honest with your expectations. Establish good communication from the get go and you will have set a solid foundation for the two of you to settle down together.

Health

Watch out for blood and stomach-related problems this year as these problems can become intrusive to the flow of your daily life. Potential ailments include indigestion or food poisoning. Get a diagnosis and treatment from your doctor early on to minimise the potential effects of these illnesses.

Career

There may be many good news at your workplace this year in the form of some sort of career advancement. That being said, do not lose sight of your physical and mental health in your excitement to pursue these opportunities too impulsively. You will need to manage your time carefully so that your workload is balanced and doable.

農曆正月

(February 4th - March 4th) 甲寅

This month, you will see your efforts finally pay off as you gain recognition and wealth as rewards for the hard work you have put into your work.

農曆二月

(March 5th - April 4th) 乙卯

Your luck with wealth continues this month. Make the most of this situation and stay diligent. Men will have better luck in potentially meeting a romantic partner this month.

農曆三月

(April 5th - May 4th) 丙辰

This is a good month for women in terms of romance. You may have to rethink your standards and expectations in such a way that you become more open with your prospects. Do not judge too harshly and you will be pleasantly surprised.

農曆四月

(May 5th - June 5th) 丁巳

Relationship problems will be a source of constant stress this month. Take a breather and think about the issues carefully so that you find a more rational and calm solution to your problems. Do not let these issues affect your work life.

農曆五月

(June 6th - July 6th) 戊午

You will experience a surge of creative energy this month and as such be able to churn out fresh ideas. These ideas can be turned into opportunities that generate financial return if you step up and take the lead in working on these ideas.

農曆六月

(July 7th - August 6th) 己未

You may find yourself embarking on quite a few travels this month. While this is a beneficial experience, you will need to be careful with the hygiene of the food that you consume so that you do not become an inadvertent victim of food poisoning.

農曆七月

(August 7th - September 7th) 庚申

Do not let your emotions get the better of you this month as you are in quite a volatile state of mind. Refrain from losing your temper or else the people around you may become turned off by your negative energy.

農曆八月

(September 8th - October 7th) 辛酉

It is not your responsibility to solve everyone's problems even if you are the leadership figure of your group. It is alright to detach yourself from their chaos and take a more passive approach.

農曆九月

(October 8th - November 6th) 壬戌

Married couples may experience a series of domestic upheavals this month. They will need to take these challenges on with understanding and patience to prevent the situation from escalating and worsening.

農曆十月

(November 7th - December 6th) 癸亥

You will need to work harder this month as the competition at your workplace is heating up and there is a threat of others overtaking you.

農曆十一月

(December 7th 2018 - January 4th 2019) 甲子

The competitive atmosphere at your workplace continues on. As the pressure builds up you will feel like lashing out, but you should refrain from such a negative reaction. Avoid shortcuts or other unethical behaviours. Take this as a learning step and be mindful of your future.

農曆十二月

(January 5th - February 3rd 2019) 乙丑

Do not neglect your relationships in favour of work. Make some time to be with your significant other or your friends. Try some fun activities that you have always wanted to experience and you will find that the experience brings you closer together.

己卯 **Ji Mao Day**

己
Ji

卯
Mao

Overview

This will be an auspicious year that you can look forward to. Your wealth will have accumulated due to your real estate investments. Additionally, you are very likely to move into a new home or acquire a new property. In short, this is a very favourable year for you to grow your wealth, with enough time and effort invested into each investment to make them truly count.

 Wealth

Your wealth prospects this year are splendid. Make sure you make use of all the opportunities that are available to you prudently and save as much money as you can. Take the time to build a strong foundation for your finances and investments, so that in the future you will have many more opportunities to earn more money.

 Relationships

Single men are likely to find this to be a rewarding year for romance as you may meet your ideal life partner. However, those who are already married should beware of disruptions in your marriage. Deal with these issues before they escalate. Single women will find that their most auspicious time for love will be during the autumn.

 Health

This year is likely to be emotionally turbulent. You will need to counter the stress you are feeling by participating in activities such as yoga that encourage wellness of the mind and soul. Be more introspective to help alleviate your more stressful thoughts. If you are above the age of forty, you should run some tests on your heart.

 Career

Your career prospects are looking good this year, though only if you work with others. Forge stronger relationships with your team, so that the support you receive from your colleagues will better equip you to meet the challenges ahead. Your peers will also be a source of different and useful perspectives on many issues.

農曆正月

(February 4th - March 4th) 甲寅
Let your ambitious side shine through this month by seizing opportunities and not being afraid to start new partnerships and develop new ideas.

農曆二月

(March 5th - April 4th) 乙卯
You have the opportunity to make some money on the side this month, thanks to the good tips and ideas provided to you by your friends.

農曆三月

(April 5th - May 4th) 丙辰
You may be prone to injuries in the leg this month, particularly on and around your knees and ankles. Be careful when exercising and performing other physical activities.

農曆四月

(May 5th - June 5th) 丁巳
Get ready to spend on your health this month. You can prevent this by successfully avoiding sharp objects that may potentially cause injury.

農曆五月

(June 6th - July 6th) 戊午
People who have been employed for a long time will find that this is a good month for them to ask for more benefits or even a raise.

農曆六月

(July 7th - August 6th) 己未
Make sure you to think before you speak this month, as your words may be offensive to others. It is best not to speak if you are unsure of others' sensitivities.

農曆七月

(August 7th - September 7th) 庚申
Do not dwell too long on things you have no control over or you will risk getting held back from taking action and moving forward.

農曆八月

(September 8th - October 7th) 辛酉
There could be disharmony at home that you will have to work hard to deal with as a result of many disagreements.

農曆九月

(October 8th - November 6th) 壬戌
You need to be wary about who you share your ideas with this month, as there is a chance that people may try to steal your ideas.

農曆十月

(November 7th - December 6th) 癸亥
Hold back on your impulses and emotions, especially during decision-making, otherwise you may jump the gun and come to a result you will later regret.

農曆十一月

(December 7th 2018 - January 4th 2019) 甲子
This is a good time to take a break from work as the stress has been plaguing you.

農曆十二月

(January 5th - February 3rd 2019) 乙丑
Sort out the problems that crop up this month as immediately as possible. Allowing them to drag out will result in long term negative effects.

庚辰 Geng Chen Day

Overview

You will be faced with new obstacles at work this year. This is mostly due to the fact that you are moving up the career ladder and thus having new experiences. You will need to hold your ground and persevere, being more pro-active in find solutions to these new problems. You will need to learn how to exercise leadership in problem solving as well.

Wealth

It will be a difficult path to wealth this year. However, you should not lose heart or focus. Even when other people fail to meet their end of the bargain, you should move on quickly and stay grounded on what your goals are. Do not dwell on the past; rather, look to the future and how you can lay a solid foundation for it.

Relationships

You will need to be more attentive to your relationship so that you prevent your bond from deteriorating. Try to see the bright side of things – that this is an opportunity for you to grow closer as a couple. Men in particular should not prioritize their work over their relationship too often.

Health

You will have less health concerns to deal with this year. That being said, do be mindful of potential minor problems with your kidney or skin as there is a possibility of recurring irritations. This could be due to an allergy, and as such you should detect the causes and avoid them.

Career

This is a suitable year for a change in career to occur, especially if it has been on your mind for a while. Think ahead and be proactive when it comes to searching for new opportunities. This change will inspire in you newfound enthusiasm and purpose. Remain meticulous with your work despite the initial excitement so as to ensure continued quality in your work.

農曆正月

(February 4th - March 4th) 甲寅
Those born in the summer will be especially prone to potential backstabbers trying to undermine their plans this month.

農曆二月

(March 5th - April 4th) 乙卯
You may find yourself tempted to succumb to outbursts of anger this month. Do not let others wind you up and thus cause you to react poorly.

農曆三月

(April 5th - May 4th) 丙辰
Married couples may have to deal with coming changes to their lives this month that may bring some tension to their relationship.

農曆四月

(May 5th - June 5th) 丁巳
While you will enjoy positive Wealth Luck this month, you will still need to work hard in order to enjoy the reward.

農曆五月

(June 6th - July 6th) 戊午
Those born in the autumn or winter will enjoy positive Wealth Luck this month. Make the most of it by seizing the opportunities that come your way.

農曆六月

(July 7th - August 6th) 己未
Make sure all loose ends are tied up before pronouncing yourself finished with a project. There is a chance that you will lose out if you take things for granted. Do not let emotions get the better of you and to think carefully before making decisions.

農曆七月

(August 7th - September 7th) 庚申
A third party could be trying to intrude into your relationship this month. Be honest with your partner about how you feel and keep the lines of communication open.

農曆八月

(September 8th - October 7th) 辛酉
You will find yourself wracked with coughs, weak lungs, and other respiratory issues this month. Men searching for romance will have to deal with potential complications.

農曆九月

(October 8th - November 6th) 壬戌
You may find yourself straining with the amount of work that you have to do this month. Take some time to step back and slow down every once in a while for your own sake.

農曆十月

(November 7th - December 6th) 癸亥
You will have to grapple with potential changes to your established plans this month. Be prepared by always having backup plans ready to go.

農曆十一月

(December 7th 2018 - January 4th 2019) 甲子
Petty people may try to get the better of you this month by claiming credit for your work. Be more discerning about who you trust and share your ideas with.

農曆十二月

(January 5th - February 3rd 2019) 乙丑
Be honest with your colleagues if they have offended you instead of talking behind their backs or reacting in an overtly hostile way.

辛巳 Xin Si Day

Overview

Your year may start off rather dull and mediocre. Things may remain stagnant for a while as you begin to feel bogged down by boredom. However, there is possibility to change the direction of things if you work hard to bring some improvement to your situation. Though you may be quite stressed out from the workload, remember that you will always reap what you sow.

 ## Wealth

Do not be afraid to innovate and pursue your plans and dreams on your own terms this year. In order to solidify your position, you will need to be proactive in your approach. If you are a business-owner, be meticulous so that your services and products meet your customers' standards. You will be rewarded if you do your best.

 ## Relationships

Your romantic luck may be rather stagnant for the first six months of the year. However, things will begin looking up again after that time period. That being said, you would be better off focusing on your career as in general, this is going to be a rather difficult year for relationships. In any case, sometimes love finds you when you are not looking.

 ## Health

Prioritise the health of your heart, eyes and kidney this year, especially if you were during the autumn and winter. Take care to get your symptoms diagnosed and treated as soon as possible.

 ## Career

Your career is moving along slowly this year, leading to frustration and fatigue. This does not mean you should stop putting in effort at work as a lack of action will result in longer term stagnancy. You can use this time to gain new talents or work on existing talents so that you expand your horizons and have more options for the future.

農曆正月

(February 4th - March 4th) 甲寅
Those who were born in the winter will benefit most from establishing partnerships and networks with others this month.

農曆二月

(March 5th - April 4th) 乙卯
Prospective mothers will need to extra careful regarding their pregnancies this month as there are potential health risks.

農曆三月

(April 5th - May 4th) 丙辰
Avoid procrastination this month and instead try to remain active. You can try resetting your goals so that you start afresh and do not lose momentum.

農曆四月

(May 5th - June 5th) 丁巳
You may have to deal with substantial stress this month even as you are already grappling with a weakened mental state due to fatigue. Do watch out for your mental well-being as much as your physical one.

農曆五月

(June 6th - July 6th) 戊午
You may have to intervene on your spouse's behalf as they may be neglecting their well-being. Take some time to watch over them and make sure all is well.

農曆六月

(July 7th - August 6th) 己未
Be wary of potentially breaking the law this month. Keep the rules in mind and always try to remain ethical and honest in your work.

農曆七月

(August 7th - September 7th) 庚申
Those who were born in the autumn and winter will have to watch out for their digestive system as there is a chance of potential health issues.

農曆八月

(September 8th - October 7th) 辛酉
Competition at the workplace surges this month, meaning that you will need to stay alert and guard against potential rivals who may be trying to overtake you or spread rumours.

農曆九月

(October 8th - November 6th) 壬戌
You may find yourself bogged down by negative feelings this month. Spend more time with your loved ones so that they can help you ease your worries.

農曆十月

(November 7th - December 6th) 癸亥
Your stomach may be the prime area for potential health issues this month. Be more mindful of what you eat so as to curb problems such as stomach flu or food poisoning.

農曆十一月

(December 7th 2018 - January 4th 2019) 甲子
Engage with your colleagues to form networks and improve your teamwork. Having their support in the event of issues with your superiors will be helpful.

農曆十二月

(January 5th - February 3rd 2019) 乙丑
It will be important for you to keep your personal life and your work life separate so that you do not bring your domestic problems to the office.

壬午 **Ren Wu Day**

Overview

Now is the time for you move on to new beginnings and forget the mistakes of the past. Your career advancement prospects are bright right now and all kinds of opportunities will come your way. If you are a business owner, this will be a good time to pursue a joint venture or partnership. However, men especially will be less romantically fortunate. It will be important for you to be more considerate in your relationship in order to preserve it.

Wealth

This year, auspicious wealth opportunities will come in the form of partnerships or teamwork. Try to work with others whenever possible even if the resulting revenue will be shared between everyone, as your cut will be more than adequate without all the accompanying stress of working alone. Work on cultivating your social network as much as you can.

Relationships

Single women will experience Peach Blossom Luck at work this year. However, it may not last long, and as such you should still seek out the opportunity to find who is truly the one for you. Single men are likely to find suitable prospects among your friends. However, married men may face difficulties in their marriage largely due to external forces influencing your wife and causing suspicion to creep into your relationship.

Health

Your eyes and heart may face some issues, though you will by and large be in good physical condition this year. However, you may gain weight which can lead to serious health issues. Make it a priority to eat healthier and have a fitness routine.

Career

While this is not be a promising year for your career, your prospects are still greater than those of last year. You may face some occasional bumps along the road, but you should treat those as a learning experience. Always be quick to make the most of the opportunities that crop up this year and work with others to exploit the benefits of teamwork.

農曆正月

(February 4th - March 4th) 甲寅
This is not a good month for women in terms of romance, as there is a third party trying to find a way to get to your partner behind your back.

農曆二月

(March 5th - April 4th) 乙卯
You will need to work on your tact and diplomacy, especially when dealing with your boss. It may be wiser for you to stay quiet rather than to cause an upheaval.

農曆三月

(April 5th - May 4th) 丙辰
You may find yourself disagreeing with colleagues frequently this month. Despite your difference, you should still keep things civil and prioritise compromise.

農曆四月

(May 5th - June 5th) 丁巳
You may have many social obligations this month, though you should resist the urge to party too much, or you may burn out from exhaustion and compromise your work.

農曆五月

(June 6th - July 6th) 戊午
Men may find themselves facing many personal problems this month, as the women in your life are infighting. It will be best to let things cool off by themselves.

農曆六月

(July 7th - August 6th) 己未
Take your challenges in stride this month or you may find yourself stumbling over your own feet and making worse mistakes.

農曆七月

(August 7th - September 7th) 庚申
Try to stay focused and grounded, especially if you want to keep your remaining good Wealth Luck for the rest of this month.

農曆八月

(September 8th - October 7th) 辛酉
You may find yourself plagued by some health issues with your liver, especially if you are someone who drinks a lot of alcohol. Exercise moderation as the risk is not worth the temporary satisfaction.

農曆九月

(October 8th - November 6th) 壬戌
Your partner may have to deal with some legal issues this month, though you need to be careful with how you get involved.

農曆十月

(November 7th - December 6th) 癸亥
There is a possibility of stomach flu and food poisoning plaguing you this month, especially if you are travelling.

農曆十一月

(December 7th 2018 - January 4th 2019) 甲子
Many friends and relatives may come to you for help with finances. However, do not be coerced into helping if you cannot afford it.

農曆十二月

(January 5th - February 3rd 2019) 乙丑
You may fall prey to overindulgence this month, which can lead to overspending. As such, you will need to make sure you exercise discipline and caution.

癸未 Gui Wei Day

Overview

The key to getting through a period of uncertainty and stagnancy is to team up with trusted peers. You will need to manage your team well in order to achieve success and recognition. You will need to solidify your relationships and accumulate an extensive social network. Be less stubborn about your methods and ideas, and instead try to be more accommodating and adaptable.

 ## Wealth

Your Wealth Luck is looking good this year, but this does not mean there will be competition. Travel will be auspicious for you, though you should do your research and plan, especially if investments are involved. Be more prudent with your expenses and instead save your money and invest only when your wealth prospects have improved.

 ## Relationships

You may feel intense jealousy this year as someone you have been seeing for a long time may begin directing their attentions to someone else. Do not be too disappointed by this as everyone finds their life partner in due time. If you are married, be careful not to allow your friends to influence you or be affected by gossip that could disrupt your marriage.

 ## Health

If you are more than forty years old this year, you should begin controlling your sugar intake and cholesterol levels. Take precautionary steps such as getting a full medical check-up to deter future problems and learn how to stay healthy.

 ## Career

Remain patient regarding your career progression as good things will come to you eventually. You will have a fruitful year if you are involved with in sales or work that requires travelling. However, be prepared for some fierce rivalry which may potentially turn into a partnership.

農曆正月

(February 4th - March 4th) 甲寅
Swallow your pride and admit that someone else has better ideas than yours so as to ensure that you always give your best to the project at hand.

農曆二月

(March 5th - April 4th) 乙卯
You may be thinking about switching jobs, but make sure you think your decision through carefully as there is a chance your emotions are getting to you.

農曆三月

(April 5th - May 4th) 丙辰
Be more proactive at the workplace this month and work hard to seize the opportunities that come your way.

農曆四月

(May 5th - June 5th) 丁巳
You may want to rethink how you work and what your priorities are. This may be a much-needed change that brings better results.

農曆五月

(June 6th - July 6th) 戊午
Plan well for the future to make sure future actions will be as fruitful as possible, as spontaneity may not bring about any solid impact.

農曆六月

(July 7th - August 6th) 己未
Though you may not realise it, some of your words or actions may offend others this month. As such, make sure you tread with caution.

農曆七月

(August 7th - September 7th) 庚申
Your Wealth Luck is looking better this month. Single men will also find that this is a good month for romantic endeavours.

農曆八月

(September 8th - October 7th) 辛酉
Your hard work and talent will eventually bring about solid results this month, so be sure continue persisting in your hard work.

農曆九月

(October 8th - November 6th) 壬戌
There is a possibility of a new relationship blossoming for you. However, women starting a new relationship may want to be more discreet about this information.

農曆十月

(November 7th - December 6th) 癸亥
Your wealth luck is looking up this month, though your health is not. Do not neglect your own well-being for the sake of pursuing wealth.

農曆十一月

(December 7th 2018 - January 4th 2019) 甲子
Do not lash out at your spouse due to feelings of suspicion and anger. Instead, work out your conflict amiably by being honest, patient and rational.

農曆十二月

(January 5th - February 3rd 2019) 乙丑
You may find yourself dealing with severe doubts this month, making it difficult for you to decide on anything. You can always turn to your friends to be your confidants to help you.

甲申 Jia Shen Day

Overview

This year, you will have to learn to face your challenges head on, especially those of a monetary nature. You will need to work hard and smart this year so that you can benefit from your labour and be rewarded handsomely. Try to find new ways of doing things so that you refresh your engines and prevent stagnation.

 ## Wealth

Your wealth prospects are mediocre. As such, you will need to work on saving or investing your money for the future and be careful not to spend what you make too quickly. Think ahead and have contingency plans in place.

 ## Relationships

This year is likely to be a challenging year for love there is a minor possibility for extra-marital affairs to occur. You must proceed with caution and control your desires. You will need to exercise restraint and wisdom in dealing with potentially delicate situations.

 ## Health

There is chance that you will suffer from anxiety in the face of your many responsibilities. Make sure you take some time out to relax and pace yourself. Also, keep an eye on your liver as well as potential heart problems.

 ## Career

You will need to step up your game in terms of how hard you work. Keep your head down and focus on the tasks at hand. The size of your rewards will be proportionate to the effort that you put in. As such, always keep the bigger picture in mind as you tough it out at the workplace this year.

農曆正月

(February 4th - March 4th) 甲寅
There is a likelihood that you will make some extra income this month, but make sure you do so ethically.

農曆二月

(March 5th - April 4th) 乙卯
Watch your words and actions this month because they have the potential to seriously hurt others.

農曆三月

(April 5th - May 4th) 丙辰
Make sure you keep the momentum going this month and stay ahead of everyone else by looking for new experiences and diversifying your talents.

農曆四月

(May 5th - June 5th) 丁巳
You may face some minor health issues this month, and as such, you will need to re-evaluate your diet and see if you can lead a healthier lifestyle.

農曆五月

(June 6th - July 6th) 戊午
Your emotions are chaotic this month. Arguments at home and at work may worsen your mental well-being. Try to take some time off to look inward and understand your emotions.

農曆六月

(July 7th - August 6th) 己未
Relatives and friends may come to you for help this month. Be honest with your ability to help, and tactfully decline if you truly cannot.

農曆七月

(August 7th - September 7th) 庚申
Keep your eye on the prize and focus on the task at hand. Make sure you utilize your abilities fully and do not let your emotions get in the way of your goals.

農曆八月

(September 8th - October 7th) 辛酉
Be careful of your alcohol intake this month, especially if you find yourself attending many social activities. Always watch your words and actions in public.

農曆九月

(October 8th - November 6th) 壬戌
Your Indirect Wealth Luck is strong this month and as such you will be able to gain returns from smaller investments and side projects.

農曆十月

(November 7th - December 6th) 癸亥
Try not to finalise any financial decisions this month as this is not a good time for such a demanding activity.

農曆十一月

(December 7th 2018 - January 4th 2019) 甲子
Speeding tickets are a possible threat this month if you do not drive carefully and abide by the rules while on the road.

農曆十二月

(January 5th - February 3rd 2019) 乙丑
You will be given recognition at work for your efforts and talents. Keep up the momentum and you may just land a promotion eventually.

乙酉 **Yi You Day**

Overview

Unforeseen circumstances will cause chaos is your year. Where you were expecting smooth sailing, you may be caught off guard and forced to adapt. As such, it is advisable for you to lay low and focus on planning for the next year without using too much time this year to make too many moves. You can see this as downtime to acquire new skills and explore new avenues in life.

 Wealth

You should jump at the opportunity to travel abroad for your work as they will result in great rewards and new experiences that will enrich your life. Be careful with your finances especially if you are in a relationship to avoid complications and misunderstandings.

 Relationships

This may be a difficult year for married couples as your patience with your partner will be tested. If you fail to resolve disputes amicably, there is a chance of splitting up. Fights should not be allowed to escalate out of reason and mutual understanding. You must work together to repair the cracks and talk things through. Surviving this trying time will mean coming out stronger as a couple. Single individuals will find that this will likely be a fruitless year for starting a relationship.

 Health

Do not take things for granted and assume that medical check-ups are unnecessary. Prevention is always better than cure and it is better to diagnose any possible ailments early on so that you have enough time to deal with it.

 Career

There will be financial opportunities hidden within your work trips this year. Keep your eyes peeled for possible opportunities and try to be proactive so as to make the most of your time abroad. If there is no opportunity to travel, your career progress will likely be stagnant for a while.

農曆正月

(February 4th - March 4th) 甲寅
Those born during the autumn will find that their financial wealth greatly improves this month.

農曆二月

(March 5th - April 4th) 乙卯
Your luck with wealth will continue on this month. However, aside from this you do not seem to be enjoying much fortune in other areas of your life.

農曆三月

(April 5th - May 4th) 丙辰
You will find yourself bogged down by a series of obstacles keeping you from your pursuits. Instead of acting out in frustration, be humble in accepting that everyone has to go through a learning curve.

農曆四月

(May 5th - June 5th) 丁巳
There may be unexpected revelations in terms of your relationships, with some sort of betrayal coming to light. Married women are especially prone to this possibility.

農曆五月

(June 6th - July 6th) 戊午
Competition heats up at work this month with the pressure building for you to show yourself at your best. This may lead you to want to take things on alone and show off, however this will do you no good as you will eventually burn out.

農曆六月

(July 7th - August 6th) 己未
You will need to reset your expectations of life a little bit this month as there are disappointments in store for you. Try to be more realistic and open to other possibilities.

農曆七月

(August 7th - September 7th) 庚申
Luck is on your side this month as you find yourself an excellent partner for business or your career. They will be an effective communicator and trusted friend.

農曆八月

(September 8th - October 7th) 辛酉
This is a good month for you to travel. Do not be overexcited by the potential adventure and you're your guard down, forgetting to watch out for your own health and safety. Take particular care with food as there is a risk of stomach flu or food poisoning.

農曆九月

(October 8th - November 6th) 壬戌
Be careful with your personal documents and property this month as it is likely that their safety is at risk this month.

農曆十月

(November 7th - December 6th) 癸亥
Those born during autumn will be blessed with good luck this month. You can go ahead and act more aggressively in pursuing your goals as it is likely that good results will come your way.

農曆十一月

(December 7th 2018 - January 4th 2019) 甲子
Be more patient and careful when signing deals concerning real estate this month. Do not let the excitement of the proceedings get to you and cloud your judgment as rushing will result in poor decisions.

農曆十二月

(January 5th - February 3rd 2019) 乙丑
This is a suitable month for travelling, as the activity will bring you luck. Remember to be carefule and watchful when you are in a foreign land so that you respect their laws and customs.

丙戌 **Bing Xu Day**

Overview

This will be a fruitful year for you as your career progresses well and many opportunities you're your way to assist you with your goals. There is a chance you may even get the chance to work at a bigger and more prestigious company, one that you have always wanted to join.

 ### Wealth

You may find yourself gaining a significant fortune during the first half of the year. However, true wealth will only come after you have put in the proper effort that will lead to power, authority and reputation. Press on with your efforts at work to gain your due benefits.

 ### Relationships

If you are single, it is likely that you will meet someone to your liking. However, married couples should watch out for problems as they may find themselves locking heads with their spouse to the point of frequent and unhealthy arguments.

 ### Health

Your health is likely to be in good condition this year due to the fact that you have been diligent in taking care of your well-being. Be mindful of your diet as you may be prone to digestive disorders and other minor issues such as food poisoning towards the end of the year, especially if you were born in the winter.

 ### Career

This is an opportune time for you to move up in your position at the workplace. Work to impress your boss with your fresh ideas leadership skills. Be on the lookout for better job opportunities as there is also the likelihood that others are interested in what you have to offer.

農曆正月

(February 4th - March 4th) 甲寅
Your Financial Luck is strong this month, due to the bright ideas you have been able to come up with and capitalise on so far.

農曆二月

(March 5th - April 4th) 乙卯
You will continue to enjoy favourable Wealth Luck this month. As such, use this time to your advantage and work on closing as many deals as possible.

農曆三月

(April 5th - May 4th) 丙辰
Work on forming a strong bond with your superiors this month to clinch their future support of your ideas and work.

農曆四月

(May 5th - June 5th) 丁巳
Do not let yourself get distracted and prone to procrastination this month as this will not do you any favours.

農曆五月

(June 6th - July 6th) 戊午
It is likely that you may receive a promotion this month, or even a job offer at a different workplace.

農曆六月

(July 7th - August 6th) 己未
You may feel the desire to switch things up and try something new. Take this chance to acquire some fresh skills or talents.

農曆七月

(August 7th - September 7th) 庚申
Work-related travel may be a possibility this month and may even occur in frequency. This may become a problem for your spouse if you are married.

農曆八月

(September 8th - October 7th) 辛酉
This month, do not let petty rumours distract you from what is important. Ignore unscrupulous gossips and stay focused.

農曆九月

(October 8th - November 6th) 壬戌
You will be blessed with much positive energy this month, and as such, you will be able to channel this into doing some good work. Simply make sure you avoid conflict with your superiors.

農曆十月

(November 7th - December 6th) 癸亥
An opportunity for a partnership may come your way this month, but now is not a good time for you to pursue this. Leave the decision for a more auspicious time.

農曆十一月

(December 7th 2018 - January 4th 2019) 甲子
There may be people who are trying to catch you unawares and claim your ideas as their own. As such, you will need to be careful about who you trust with such information.

農曆十二月

(January 5th - February 3rd 2019) 乙丑
Health issues may plague you this month due to the stress you have been combatting as a result of your busy work schedule. Take some time off for a holiday to rejuvenate and recuperate.

丁亥 Ding Hai Day

Overview
The coming year will be a good time for you to think about the future and work on the direction you are heading. This period of introspection serves as a way to better understand yourself better so that you craft your actions and goals around your abilities. This will help you stay focused and realistic. On a different note, you will probably face some relationship issues this year which will require you to manage your emotions properly. Wealth-wise, look to property for better returns.

Wealth
Your Wealth Luck this year will be rather average, and there is even a likelihood you may lose some money. Manage your finances better and opt for sound property investments instead, for which you should do your homework and invest wisely. Otherwise, you risk suffering legal problems and subsequently even more financial losses.

Relationships
Single women have the luck to find a romantic partner this year. You will have plenty of opportunities to meet interesting people, just be careful that do you do not lead others on in your pursuit of dating. In contrast, married men will have quite a bit of trouble to deal with.

Health
Your health is likely to be stable unless you were born in the winter. In that case, take care of your immune system. Focus on improving your health in small ways that can be incorporated into your daily life, such switching to a healthier diet, exercising, and taking proper care of yourself if you fall ill.

Career
Those who work in the creative industry are likely to enjoy a productive and inspiring year. A promotion and travel opportunity are also likely. Travelling will maintain your momentum and broaden your opportunities.

農曆正月

(February 4th - March 4th) 甲寅
This month sees an increase of wealth opportunities, largely due to the many good ideas you produce that will be met with enthusiasm at your workplace.

農曆二月

(March 5th - April 4th) 乙卯
This month brings you strong Indirect Wealth Luck, which will help you reap rewards on the side from investments and other projects.

農曆三月

(April 5th - May 4th) 丙辰
You may get a promotion or other career advancement opportunities this month that will bring you great benefits.

農曆四月

(May 5th - June 5th) 丁巳
There is a possibility of travel this month, during which you should be careful when interpreting the law in a foreign country.

農曆五月

(June 6th - July 6th) 戊午
You will have strong Wealth Luck this month which you should capitalise on by seizing all opportunities.

農曆六月

(July 7th - August 6th) 己未
You may find yourself troubled by certain issues this month, though you need to remember to keep your cool when deciding how to act on it.

農曆七月

(August 7th - September 7th) 庚申
There will be some intense rivalry at the workplace this month and as such, you will need to protect your interests while maintaining cordial relationships with your peers.

農曆八月

(September 8th - October 7th) 辛酉
There is a possibility that some of the ideas you have been developing will be poached by colleagues who are trying to take credit for your work.

農曆九月

(October 8th - November 6th) 壬戌
Pay attention to your physical health this month by exercising more and maintaining a healthy diet.

農曆十月

(November 7th - December 6th) 癸亥
Patience is an important virtue to cultivate this month. Avoid rushing into things, especially when it comes to money.

農曆十一月

(December 7th 2018 - January 4th 2019) 甲子
There will be some issues that you will need to address at the workplace through clear and honest communication with your peers and bosses.

農曆十二月

(January 5th - February 3rd 2019) 乙丑
This is a month of action. Avoid hesitation and too much time spent contemplating as these will lead to procrastination.

戊子 Wu Zi Day

Overview

You will be blessed with a plethora of opportunities this year that can be readily and effectively exploited to bring great progress in your life. However, buried demons from your past may resurface as legal issues. You will further be challenged by the stress of trying to work at your goals, which will prove detrimental to your well-being. As such, you will need to manage your resources and energy wisely.

 ## Wealth

It is very likely that you will make a fortune this year. However, there may be more to these opportunities than meets the eye so you will need to remain prudent. Do not cut corners or neglect ethics in order to make money. The legal problems that will arise as a result are not worth it. Stay cautious to avoid potential trouble.

 ## Relationships

Men will find this to be an emotionally turbulent year. However, you have a chance to survive the issues in your relationship and come out stronger. Women on the other hand will need to seek balance between romance and everything else. Do not prioritise your relationship at the expense of the other aspects of your life.

 ## Health

This year, your liver is the centre of your health problems. Manage your alcohol intake and be extremely cautious about your health in general. Do also watch out for growths or tumours.

 ## Career

Those born in the spring will have good career prospects. Bear in mind that it is alright and sometimes even necessary to ask for help, without having to singularly shoulder the burden of carrying everything on your own. Others will be willing to lend a helping hand and will greatly ease your path.

農曆正月

(February 4th - March 4th) 甲寅

Your colleagues will end up being a comforting and resourceful source of help to you this month. Take in their ideas with an open mind and work together to execute them.

農曆二月

(March 5th - April 4th) 乙卯

Women will face some gynaecological issues. To prevent it from becoming more serious over time, you should seek help from a professional.

農曆三月

(April 5th - May 4th) 丙辰

Both your work and relationships will experience stagnancy this month. Do not be passive regarding your situation, but rather work on getting yourself back on track.

農曆四月

(May 5th - June 5th) 丁巳

You will be tempted to take shortcuts and ignore ethics to get what you want. However, you should maintain the lest you regret your discrepancies.

農曆五月

(June 6th - July 6th) 戊午

Those born in the spring will find that this is a good month for career advancement. Those who were born in the other seasons will inversely have to deal with stress.

農曆六月

(July 7th - August 6th) 己未

Health issues are your main focus this month and as such you should keep an eye on your physical well-being. There may be a possible trip to the dentist.

農曆七月

(August 7th - September 7th) 庚申

Now is a good time for you to keep pushing on to learn new things and expand your horizons. Seek out opportunities to gain knowledge, such as short courses and workshops, and you will find that your life becomes more interesting.

農曆八月

(September 8th - October 7th) 辛酉

Do not let impulse rules your decisions this month. Make sure you think carefully before doing anything to avoid later negative results.

農曆九月

(October 8th - November 6th) 壬戌

Be wary of the motives of people who may appear too good to be true. Some of them may be insincere and are trying to get the better of you.

農曆十月

(November 7th - December 6th) 癸亥

This is a good month for travel, especially to the south. Make the effort to go on this trip for valuable new experiences and ideas.

農曆十一月

(December 7th 2018 - January 4th 2019) 甲子

You will find yourself faced with tension in your relationship this month. Jealousy and insecurity are at the root of your problems, and as such you will need to be more trusting and carefree.

農曆十二月

(January 5th - February 3rd 2019) 乙丑

This is a month for you to wind down and relax. You deserve a break, so make the most of your down time and enjoy yourself.

己丑 Ji Chou Day

Overview

This will be a rather uneventful year without strong showings in luck. Those born in the autumn are advised to be more prudent and cautious due to the possibility of being tangled up in legal issues. In addition, do not shy away from collaborations and social activities as it is more favourable for you to engage in groups rather than try to go solo. Do have some funds available as there is a possibility you may have to fork out some money for an unforeseen health problem.

 Wealth

Your wealth luck is in a generally good place. However, you will need to hone your patience in focusing on minor details, as one small misstep can result in unfavourable situations. Do not settle for shortcuts just because you are lazy. You will need to work hard in order to maintain your place.

 Relationships

Your romantic prospects are in an upswing this year, especially for single individuals. However, those who are married will find themselves possibly caught up with extramarital affairs. Do not allow yourself to be tempted by such temporary pleasures as this will result in the collapse of your relationship.

 Health

There is a chance that you will have to endure surgery this year. Thankfully, it is only a minor one that you will be able to pull through with a little bit of rest on your side. Make sure you prioritize your health over other more trivial aspects of your life as there is a possibility that you may also be faced with stomach-related problems. Do not to take things for granted and remember that prevention is better than cure.

 Career

You will enjoy substantial luck with your career this year, especially if you were born during the spring. Everyone else will be faced with the stress of increased workloads, which may result in anxiety and unhappiness. Spend some time for yourself relaxing and recollecting your thoughts.

農曆正月

(February 4th - March 4th) 甲寅
Others will challenge your position and ideas this month, so be prepared to stand up for yourself and strive to push for what you planned for.

農曆二月

(March 5th - April 4th) 乙卯
You may be plagued by a sore throat or fever this month, especially if you were born in the summer.

農曆三月

(April 5th - May 4th) 丙辰
Financial opportunities will come to you this month that can result in great rewards. Do keep in mind that this will require teamwork and assistance from others.

農曆四月

(May 5th - June 5th) 丁巳
Those born in the spring may experience positive career luck. There is a possibility that they may receive a pay raise or promotion.

農曆五月

(June 6th - July 6th) 戊午
You will experience substantial stress through your work this month due to increased responsibilities given to you. Do try to manage your time properly so that you do not end up overworking.

農曆六月

(July 7th - August 6th) 己未
There is a likelihood of surgery this month. Do not be too alarmed. Instead, make sure you discuss the procedures and options carefully with your doctor so that you are confident in the process.

農曆七月

(August 7th - September 7th) 庚申
You will find yourself fighting battles at work alone. Do not give in to laziness or procrastination as you will only be accumulating your stress.

農曆八月

(September 8th - October 7th) 辛酉
Be careful with tools or other potentially harmful implements this month as there is a possibility that you may injure yourself.

農曆九月

(October 8th - November 6th) 壬戌
Hone your delegating skills so that you spread your work out among others. This way, you can generate more productivity for less stress.

農曆十月

(November 7th - December 6th) 癸亥
It is time for you to embark on that vacation that you have been awaiting. It is good to pay off your hard work and dedication with some well-earned time off.

農曆十一月

(December 7th 2018 - January 4th 2019) 甲子
Your ideas will bring you positive financial results this month. Do not be afraid to take the first step to realize your plans.

農曆十二月

(January 5th - February 3rd 2019) 乙丑
Make sure you spend wisely and keep your frugality this month. Try to save whenever you can. Impulse spending will bring about a long-term negative effect to your wealth.

庚寅 Geng Yin Day

Overview
You will have much unforeseen opportunities to work with in your career this year. You will have to be adaptable and ready to make new plans in order to make the most of your opportunities. You can cultivate your talents by learning new skills and experimenting with new ideas. For business owners, it is important to innovate your methods to yield better results.

Wealth
You may want to consider investing in some assets this year, as it is favourable to do so. In order to keep your finances in check, plan out a budget and stick to it as best you can. Work to resist the urge to spend impulsively. Make sure to invest only in that which will bring returns.

Relationships
Men will have more Peach Blossom Luck than women this year. Hence, women need to be prepared for their relationships to be tested to its limits. You should take this time to determine if the relationship is worth fighting for by using your wisdom and fortitude.

Health
You will have a great health outlook this year, but do not take it for granted. Some allergies are likely to occur with food or your skin. Although these are likely to be minor, it pays to be vigilant towards your diet. Hence, you will need to map out a health plan that involves both your diet and exercise.

Career
This will be the right time to switch careers, especially if you have already gained recognition for your talents and capabilities. Your ideas will be well-known if you make sure to promote them. As such, you will need to work on improving your communication and presentation skills. That being said, your temper is rather volatile, especially where your boss is concerned. As such, you will need to try your best to remain diplomatic and peaceful.

農曆正月

(February 4th - March 4th) 甲寅
This will not be an auspicious month for your wealth in particular, and as such you should try to think of new ways to generate profit.

農曆二月

(March 5th - April 4th) 乙卯
Try to turn your adversaries into your collaborators this month, as sometimes the worst enemies can become the greatest friends.

農曆三月

(April 5th - May 4th) 丙辰
Do not let yourself be left behind by the current. Even though procrastination may be tempting, it will only set you back.

農曆四月

(May 5th - June 5th) 丁巳
You may have a short temper this month, and as such, you should try to watch your emotional outbursts. That being said, you will enjoy Wealth Luck.

農曆五月

(June 6th - July 6th) 戊午
Focusing too much on your wealth will only bring detriment to your personal relationships this month as you are likely to neglect them.

農曆六月

(July 7th - August 6th) 己未
Men who have been in long-term relationships you may find that this is a good month to take things to the next level and settle down.

農曆七月

(August 7th - September 7th) 庚申
You will need to seek out encouragement and support from your superiors in order to be able to acquire wealth in the future.

農曆八月

(September 8th - October 7th) 辛酉
You may find yourself rewarded with a potential promotion at work or a pay raise this month.

農曆九月

(October 8th - November 6th) 壬戌
This is a good month for you in terms of a heightened momentum and desire to discover new things.

農曆十月

(November 7th - December 6th) 癸亥
You will likely be travelling this month, although you may suffer from minor health issues such as food allergies or stomach flu.

農曆十一月

(December 7th 2018 - January 4th 2019) 甲子
Ignore the temptation to overspend this month, as it will only result in financial regrets.

農曆十二月

(January 5th - February 3rd 2019) 乙丑
People at work may come up with some good ideas this month to help you along and as such you will need to have an open mind and keep your ears perked up.

辛卯 **Xin Mao Day**

Overview

You will find yourself finally blessed with the recognition and popularity that you have been pursuing as your efforts and talents are noticed. Despite this, you will have some trouble accumulating with your finances, especially if you were born during the spring or summer. Do not take this too harshly as it opens up free time for you to plan for your future and use this as a transition period to get prepared. Travel or a change of career may provide a breath of fresh air and thus better wealth opportunities.

 ### Wealth

Despite the lack of Wealth Luck this year, there will still be other opportunities in other areas of your life. Do not waste time slaving away without satisfying returns. Do not be afraid to pull away and refocus your efforts on something more enjoyable. Creative or artistic pursuits may end up being immensely rewarding for you, possible even helping you to generate some income and providing much needed mental stimulation.

 ### Relationships

Single women are better off focusing on other areas of their life this year as pursuing romance may only result in a broken heart and waste time. Focus on other passions and interests. Give your time to your friends and family, as well as your work. On the other hand, men who are in a relationship may have to deal with the complications of an intrusive third-party who is trying to make a move on your partner.

 ### Health

Your eyes mat become a source of health problems this year, despite your generally good health. Another source of health problem is the constant stress and pressure you take in throughout the year, which may cause fatigue and depression. Always remember that your mental health is just as important as your physical health.

 ### Career

There will be an increase in your workload this year and much for you to juggle with. Your stress levels will start to peak what with all the burden on your shoulders. Do not be afraid to ask for help and share a bit of the load. You will need to be honest with yourself about what you can and cannot take so you do not end up doing too much damage to your mental health.

農曆正月

(February 4th - March 4th) 甲寅
There will be many Noble People around you this month to share their assistance and expertise. Do not be afraid to reach out and gain the friendship of good people.

農曆二月

(March 5th - April 4th) 乙卯
Those born during autumn and winter will experience good luck getting involved in various partnerships and other collaborative efforts.

農曆三月

(April 5th - May 4th) 丙辰
You may feel as if a cloud of fatigue is following you around this month. Your progress in most endeavours drags on slowly, and languor looms everywhere. Try to get involved in some activities to keep your momentum up and keep you from becoming discouraged.

農曆四月

(May 5th - June 5th) 丁巳
Your social network may become a helpful resource for business and wealth opportunities this month. Be on the lookout for this potential and do not be afraid to ask your friends for their help.

農曆五月

(June 6th - July 6th) 戊午
Muster the will to be more focused at work so that you do not become a victim of unscrupulous individuals are seeking to overtake your position or spread lies about you.

農曆六月

(July 7th - August 6th) 己未
New ideas will spring forth this month that lead you to new places in your workplace and in your life. Do not be afraid to get creative as it could bring substantial rewards.

農曆七月

(August 7th - September 7th) 庚申
Those born during the spring or summer will receive some good news at work this month most likely in the form of a career advancement opportunity.

農曆八月

(September 8th - October 7th) 辛酉
Do not let yourself get pressured into breaking the law or doing something unethical, even if it means your peers will give you trouble for it. The short term reward of earning the friendship of unscrupulous individuals is not worth the long term effects of whatever punishment you will receive for doing the wrong thing.

農曆九月

(October 8th - November 6th) 壬戌
Give yourself a break this month as a reward for having done so much work thus far.

農曆十月

(November 7th - December 6th) 癸亥
Always be mindful to think things through carefully before making a decision on complex matters that require more forethought. Do not be stubborn about discussing the issue beforehand.

農曆十一月

(December 7th 2018 - January 4th 2019) 甲子
Healthy teamwork will prove to be beneficial for you. Your relationships with your peers will be strengthened and everyone will learn valuable interpersonal skills.

農曆十二月

(January 5th - February 3rd 2019) 乙丑
You will have an increase of leisure time which you will be tempted to spend on partying. However, you should exercise some restraint and refrain from overindulging as this will reap negative results for your health.

壬辰 Ren Chen Day

Overview

This year, your community will be at the centre of your success. Make sure you pay attention to your colleagues' ideas and be your best self in the presence of mentors who can assist you in future endeavours. Furthermore, work at strengthening the bond with your community by being generous with those who are in need. This will also help you enlarge your social network and harness a good reputation, which in turn, may bring a plethora of opportunities to expand your wealth.

 ## Wealth

Most of your wealth will be made through working and investing your money with others. Make sure you do not squander your money on social outings in the pursuit of this results. Prudence is still important in managing financial matters and discerning who amongst your acquaintances are sincere and deserving.

 ## Relationships

Your Peach Blossom Luck is mediocre at best this year. If you are a woman who is already attached, you may have to contend with friends who have wicked intentions. They may cause problems to your relationship or even become the third-party. On the other hand, if you are a man who is in a relationship, you will need to pay less heed to what your friends say about your current relationship, as their words could be harmful to your relationship.

 ## Health

It is likely that you will experience headaches and migraines caused by stress this year. Hence, you will need to alleviate the factors that induce these problems. Stomach aches and food poisoning might also be a problem, so be mindful of what you eat. Managing your stress is the key to eliminating potential stomach issues and headaches this year.

 ## Career

This year, most of your opportunities will come from your professional networks. Work hard to receive recognition at work as this will help you gain credibility. That being said, remember that humility is important and you will need to remain generous in sharing the credit with others who helped you achieve your task. You can also circumvent potential workplace disputes by forging strong bonds with your colleagues.

農曆正月

(February 4th - March 4th) 甲寅
You can start off your year on the right note by building strong relationships with your co-workers or business partners, which will set the tone for many opportunities to come.

農曆二月

(March 5th - April 4th) 乙卯
Your friends may be a resource for some great ideas, and as such you should keep an open mind and be attentive to their words.

農曆三月

(April 5th - May 4th) 丙辰
Although there may be some potential conflicts with your boss this month, you should take a step back to calm down and keep up your hard work.

農曆四月

(May 5th - June 5th) 丁巳
Although you and your peers will be confident in your ideas, you will need to work hard to sell it to your sceptical boss. As such, you will need to hone your persuasion skills and strategise carefully.

農曆五月

(June 6th - July 6th) 戊午
Try to think about how you can improve your approaches to work this month, as repetitive methods may be the cause of a lack of progress.

農曆六月

(July 7th - August 6th) 己未
Compromise with your colleagues instead of trying to fight things out this month, or risk ruining relations with them in the long term.

農曆七月

(August 7th - September 7th) 庚申
If you plan to travel this month, be on the lookout for minor accidents that may occur and also watch your personal safety and belongings.

農曆八月

(September 8th - October 7th) 辛酉
This is a good month for Wealth, especially for those born in the summer. Opportunities will be plenty and you should seize them when you have the chance.

農曆九月

(October 8th - November 6th) 壬戌
There may be some problems at work in terms of feeling like your superiors are pushing you around. Make sure you stand up for yourself and seek a proper solution.

農曆十月

(November 7th - December 6th) 癸亥
Postpone important decisions this month, as you lack the clarity and focus to think straight with fluctuating emotions plaguing your mind.

農曆十一月

(December 7th 2018 - January 4th 2019) 甲子
People around you may be trying to charm you into lending them money. Make sure you know your limits so you do not lose out.

農曆十二月

(January 5th - February 3rd 2019) 乙丑
If you are a woman in a relationship, you will have to deal with the threat of a third party interfering with your relationship this month. Be sure to be attentive of suspicious activities.

癸巳 **Gui Si Day**

Overview

This is a year that favours socialization, teamwork, and collaborations. Those going for joint ventures and partnerships will indubitably obtain favourable outcomes by the end of the year. Likewise, you will also yield better results at work through teamwork and by seeking the help of your peers. Hone your social skills and build your networks so that you establish more collaborative opportunities.

 Wealth

Wealth opportunities are abundant, giving you plenty of room to expand on your wealth. The collaborations you are involved will bring you great rewards, and as such you should share the profits with those who have helped you. Now is also a good time for you to go out and find the best people to work with.

 Relationships

Try to keep relationships off your mind this year as your prospects are mediocre. Focus on other areas of your life as most of your relationship may result in you getting the short end of the stick. If you are in a relationship, be committed to fidelity and do not prioritize your work over your relationship.

 Health

Those born in the winter will have to pay more attention to their health this year. Try to get a full medical check-up to ensure that everything is as it should be. Your immune system will be rather weak, and as such you should remain on your toes to make sure your situation does not go awry too quickly.

 Career

Teamwork and joint ventures are the way to go this year. Be sure to engage others in your ideas and projects so that you have a solid base to share information and expertise. Stay on the good side of your superiors so that they too can lend their support when it is needed.

農曆正月

(February 4th - March 4th) 甲寅
Your work will start off well this month. You will have luck on your side as you approach your superiors with an idea pitch.

農曆二月

(March 5th - April 4th) 乙卯
Do not be afraid to assert your value at work and request for the appropriate acknowledgment of your hard work and talents.

農曆三月

(April 5th - May 4th) 丙辰
Teamwork will bring you great benefits at the workplace and as such, do not shy away from sharing your ideas and listening to the suggestions of others.

農曆四月

(May 5th - June 5th) 丁巳
Focus on the well-being of your stomach this month, as you may be plagued with digestive problems issues and health problems such as food poisoning.

農曆五月

(June 6th - July 6th) 戊午
Look out for your mother's health and well-being this month, as she is most at risk of a sudden health issue that may result in a hefty medical bill.

農曆六月

(July 7th - August 6th) 己未
You will need to be careful with what you say this month as your words carry the potential of hurting others. Keep your more fiery opinions to yourself.

農曆七月

(August 7th - September 7th) 庚申
Your wealth luck is in an upswing this month. Working with others will solidify this luck, bringing you great results. Make sure you give back to those who have helped you out along the way.

農曆八月

(September 8th - October 7th) 辛酉
Stress bogs you down at work this month, though you should try your best to remain unaffected. Stay strong and keep working hard.

農曆九月

(October 8th - November 6th) 壬戌
You may be potentially receiving a promotion at the workplace this month. When the time comes for your consideration, exercise a balance of both humility and confidence.

農曆十月

(November 7th - December 6th) 癸亥
Avoid making major decisions in terms of your wealth this month, as this is not the time to reorganise your finances. Do not bring about sudden changes.

農曆十一月

(December 7th 2018 - January 4th 2019) 甲子
This is a good month for socialising so that you can expand your social circles and networks. Take this opportunity to re-establish old connections and strengthen them.

農曆十二月

(January 5th - February 3rd 2019) 乙丑
You may be able to find new business deals through meeting new people. Keep an open mind but also think their suggestions through carefully.

甲午 Jia Wu Day

Overview

Creativity and inspiration is abound in your life. If you work in the creative industry, you will find many favourable opportunities come your way allowing you to showcase your new ideas. Be prepared for this challenge and do not be afraid to shine. You will need to watch out for your personal finances this year as they are in a risky state.

Wealth

There will be many opportunities for you to generate more wealth in the first half of this year. Once you gain these rewards, be careful to not waste them away on trivial expenditures. Being impulsive with your money will hold you back from making more progress later.

Relationships

Romantic luck is not on your side this year. Your attempts at finding a partner will be met with unfortunate lack of chemistry or rejection. Do not get too frustrated. Instead, just take some time off romance and focus on other things such as your career and personal passions. Love cannot be forced; you simply need to wait for the right time to find someone.

Health

You will need to focus more on stress and anger management this year as this will be quite a challenging time for you mentally. If you let stress get to you too easily, your physical health will also be affected. Separate the pressures of work from your persona life so as to not let both sides of your life get tangled up with one another.

Career

Do not wait around for opportunities to be handed to you and then complain when you do not seem to be making any progress. There will be plenty of opportunities for you to make a lasting impression if only you seize the chance. Consider enrolling in some courses to acquire new skills so that you become a more valuable asset.

農曆正月

(February 4th - March 4th) 甲寅
There may be some positive changes at your workplace this month, possibly in the form of a new superior or a salary boost.

農曆二月

(March 5th - April 4th) 乙卯
This may be a rather stressful month for you due to the burden of a heavy workload, especially if you were born in the summer. Make sure you manage your time and stress well so you do not become overwhelmed.

農曆三月

(April 5th - May 4th) 丙辰
Have more faith in your ability to get things done this month. Muster your resolve and believe in yourself as you will need to charge ahead and act in order to progress.

農曆四月

(May 5th - June 5th) 丁巳
You may find yourself bogged down by difficult dilemmas this month. Do not be afraid to go to others for their advice on the matter to ease your decision-making process.

農曆五月

(June 6th - July 6th) 戊午
Your opponents will come out in full swing to challenge you. As such you will need to rise to the occasion and counter with preparedness and strategies. This is good experience for you to learn how to resolve conflicts in the future.

農曆六月

(July 7th - August 6th) 己未
There may be disagreements at the workplace this month. Do not let it escalate out of control. Instead, face the problems with maturity and reason without letting emotions get in the way.

農曆七月

(August 7th - September 7th) 庚申
More positive changes are in store for you this month. Embrace and adapt to these changes as they will greatly improve your situation.

農曆八月

(September 8th - October 7th) 辛酉
You will need to watch out for your personal items and safety, as there is a risk of robbery this month. You may also have to combat some unexpected mood-swing.

農曆九月

(October 8th - November 6th) 壬戌
You may find it difficult to breathe, signalling a decline in respiratory health. Pay more attention to caring for your lungs and stay away from activities that damage them. Seek medical treatment as soon as you notice these symptoms.

農曆十月

(November 7th - December 6th) 癸亥
Travelling for work will bring you positive benefits. As such, you should seize the opportunity to do so and do your best to learn from the experience.

農曆十一月

(December 7th 2018 - January 4th 2019) 甲子
There may be a promotion waiting for you at work this month. However, this may cause unrest among your colleagues who are jealous of your luck. Stay away from these people who cannot be happy for you and celebrate your achievements.

農曆十二月

(January 5th - February 3rd 2019) 乙丑
You will be bothered by loneliness this month, which may be a result of you having constantly prioritized work over your relationships in the past. Take some time to reconnect with people important to you.

乙未 Yi Wei Day

Overview

Those born in the winter will find this to be a challenging year ahead as unexpected obstacles come in the way of your plans. Your personal goals may be put on hold as a result and you may find yourself becoming dejected with the results. However, do not let this affect you too harshly and instead turn your attention to your career as it has the potential to take off this year.

Wealth

Your financial outlook for the year is rather bleak. Investing is not a wise course for you to take at this time, though property is a safer bet if you absolutely must put your money somewhere. Speculation will only bring financial devastation. All money decisions you make at this time must come from careful consideration and strong planning.

Relationships

This is a good time for single men to pursue romantic relationships this year. There is a chance that your mother's social network will bring good candidates for such endeavours. Women, on the other hand, will have a harder time finding love. There is a chance that you may be too defensive and careful, which in turn makes you seem unapproachable and aloof. Consider allowing yourself to be vulnerable every now and then so that you may discover true sincerity in your partners.

Health

Your health situation appears to be moderate. You may be plagued with some heart and blood pressures issues, especially if you are over the age of forty. Do not take things for granted and make sure you go for consistent medical check-ups to prevent any escalations of health issues. There is also a possibility of eye problems that you need to be ready for.

Career

Be prudent in the decisions you make regarding and within your career this year. Do not try to juggle too many goals as they will interfere with one another and make it more difficult for you to achieve results. You will only bring yourself undue stress by spreading yourself too thin, depleting your energy and making it difficult to focus.

農曆正月

(February 4th - March 4th) 甲寅
Not all opportunities for business partnerships or joint ventures will be worth your time, no matter how attractive they seem at first. Vet your options carefully and be mindful not to jump into anything too quickly.

農曆二月

(March 5th - April 4th) 乙卯
Trouble with the law looms ahead especially for those who were born during the winter. Do not put off your problems. Instead, find solutions quickly and address your share of guilt before things get out of hand.

農曆三月

(April 5th - May 4th) 丙辰
Do not be afraid to prioritise yourself this month. Work on your confidence and do not shy away from praise, much less self-praise. There is nothing wrong with being self-assured and believing in yourself.

農曆四月

(May 5th - June 5th) 丁巳
Married individuals may face off with rumours and gossip this month regarding their relationship. However, it is best to ignore these trivial chatter and rise above the backbiting to mind your own business and work on yourself.

農曆五月

(June 6th - July 6th) 戊午
There will be Noble People around to assist you with your goals or help you out of trouble. As such, do not hesitate to ask for help and seek out other who may have more power and experience to deal with such things.

農曆六月

(July 7th - August 6th) 己未
This is a good time for co-operation between you and your peers. Collaborating with others can help lessen your workload and also bring a diversity of methods and ideas to the project so that it becomes more efficient and interesting.

農曆七月

(August 7th - September 7th) 庚申
Tension rules in workplace relationships this month. The awkward or hostile atmosphere can be alleviated through honesty and diplomacy. Problems are more easily solved when both parties communicate maturely.

農曆八月

(September 8th - October 7th) 辛酉
There will be social developments for you this month as you may find yourself seeking out new circles or heading out more. However, you should not neglect your duties or overindulge so as to ensure a balanced lifestyle.

農曆九月

(October 8th - November 6th) 壬戌
Do not leave difficult decisions to stew for too long, as important windows may close on you. Instead, keep your options open and be ready to jump on opportunities that come your way, making decisions as the path unfolds.

農曆十月

(November 7th - December 6th) 癸亥
Avoid financial decisions at this time, as it is likely that you are not in the right frame of mind to be making such significant changes in your life. Wait for a more opportune time to mull these questions over carefully.

農曆十一月

(December 7th 2018 - January 4th 2019) 甲子
Your work life may see some positive changes, maybe even in the form of a promotion before the end of the year. As such, you should maintain your workplace performance and be mindful of how you present yourself to others at work.

農曆十二月

(January 5th - February 3rd 2019) 乙丑
Vehicular or road accidents are a possibility this month, as well as running into trouble with the law. It is better to be safe than sorry and as such you should be following the rules stringently and prioritising safety above everything else.

丙申 Bing Shen Day

Bing

Shen

Overview

Stay focused on your goals as this is the perfect opportunity for growth, considering your wealth prospects for this year are good. Remain calm, rational and confident in your capabilities when you are making decisions and thinking of the next move. This will also help you deal with potential upheavals at your workplace. There may be change coming this year, in the form of a new superior or even a different career path. On a side note, travelling eastwards will benefit your wealth accumulation efforts.

 ## Wealth

Those in the education sector will find themselves granted with a better financial status. In general, your Wealth Luck will be especially strong during the first half of the year. The second half of the year will be slightly less favourable and as such you should accordingly plan ahead and be more prudent.

 ## Relationships

If you are in a steady relationship, you may want to consider settling down this year. If you are married, there is a possibility of external distractions that could disrupt your relationship. Avoid temptation and negative influence from your friends regarding your marriage.

 ## Health

Make sure you pay more attention to your well-being this year. You can prevent serious issues in the future by going for frequent medical check-ups, eating well and exercising regularly. You may be more prone to ailments relating to your digestive system in general, and as such you should watch your diet and hygiene.

 ## Career

Your work will go smoothly this year, though you will need to be more assertive in delegating tasks in the name of efficiency. Exercise good leadership by encouraging your teammates and including them in your achievements. If you play your cards right, a career advancement is likely to be in the cards this year.

農曆正月

(February 4th - March 4th) 甲寅
Your wealth luck will flourish this month if you make the most of the opportunities that come your way.

農曆二月

(March 5th - April 4th) 乙卯
Exercise more diplomacy and restraint when you are dealing with others this month. Be careful with your words or you may risk offending someone.

農曆三月

(April 5th - May 4th) 丙辰
Your turbulent emotions may cause serious discord in your life and put a stop to your plans. Do your best to moderate your emotions and avoid conflict.

農曆四月

(May 5th - June 5th) 丁巳
Stay focused on your goals to side-line feelings of isolation this month. Avoid being influenced by your emotions too much or you will be prone to overthinking.

農曆五月

(June 6th - July 6th) 戊午
People may come to you seeking financial assistance this month. If you cannot afford to be generous, do not let yourself be coerced doing something out of your ability.

農曆六月

(July 7th - August 6th) 己未
There is some tension with your boss this month which can lead to rumours from your colleagues. Speak directly with your boss to resolve your issues.

農曆七月

(August 7th - September 7th) 庚申
You're on a tipping scale of your emotions this month, clouding your mind and making it difficult to think logically.

農曆八月

(September 8th - October 7th) 辛酉
Your friends may be causing problems for you this month as there may be some individuals who are faking the friendship.

農曆九月

(October 8th - November 6th) 壬戌
Go ahead and push the envelope this month, doing something creative which will be beneficial for you and help you gain momentum.

農曆十月

(November 7th - December 6th) 癸亥
Do not be careless with the things that you say as this may cause offence to others, particularly your superiors.

農曆十一月

(December 7th 2018 - January 4th 2019) 甲子
Money could cause problems with superficial and fake people in your life who will try to use you and bring you down.

農曆十二月

(January 5th - February 3rd 2019) 乙丑
You may receive some form of career advancement this month, but there is a chance that you will have to step up and ask for it.

丁酉 Ding You Day

Overview

This year, your hard work will pay off and reward you with significant advancements. You may have the opportunity to embark on work-related travel. Use this as an opportunity to expand your social circles and lay foundations for future prospects. Do not let this get to your head and affect your ego. Students can also expect academic success if they work hard.

 ## Wealth

Be mindful of your budget this year and keep from overspending. Materialism will not bring you happiness or fulfilment, especially not when you will have to grapple with debt as a result. Any investments you make should be short term and risk free for the best results.

 ## Relationships

You will experience rocky relationships this year. The people around you will try to help with the best intentions, however, their interference will only worsen the situation. Women will have better Relationship Luck than men will. Married people should work on trust and believe in one another more than in what other people say.

 ## Health

Your health will not experience significant ups and downs this year. You may have some hearing or vision problems, but nothing that cannot be mitigated by a check-up. Blood pressure may also be an issue for individuals in their mid-thirties or older. Try to adopt a healthier lifestyle with more exercise and a better diet.

 ## Career

Individuals in the education industry will experience better career progression this year. You will need to plan carefully for your future success and establish strong relationships with your peers and superiors. Try not to offend anyone with your words and cause discord. Control your emotions and actions so that you maintain amicability with your colleagues.

農曆正月

(February 4th - March 4th) 甲寅
This month sees strong financial prospects for you. As such, you can start seeking out new ways to generate income and find wealth.

農曆二月

(March 5th - April 4th) 乙卯
Those born in the summer may be grappling with some form of minor illnesses such as a fever or sore throat.

農曆三月

(April 5th - May 4th) 丙辰
Those born in the winter may encounter positive luck in terms of their career progression this month in the form of a promotion or other bonuses.

農曆四月

(May 5th - June 5th) 丁巳
You may find your workload difficult to contend with this month. Do not get too stressed out. Instead, take things slow every now and then and have some time to yourself.

農曆五月

(June 6th - July 6th) 戊午
Your creativity will flow freely this month, bringing you innovative ideas that open up opportunities for alternative methods to generate income.

農曆六月

(July 7th - August 6th) 己未
This will be a busy month that sees you tackling stress and an increased workload. You can make things better by seeking help from your colleagues.

農曆七月

(August 7th - September 7th) 庚申
Be careful with your actions this month so that you are not too vulnerable to people who are trying to steal your ideas and take the credit for your work.

農曆八月

(September 8th - October 7th) 辛酉
Pregnant women will need to exercise extra caution this month as there is a risk of health problems. Everyone else will need to be more careful with their right side.

農曆九月

(October 8th - November 6th) 壬戌
You will be inspired to instigate some form of change in your life. Do not be scared to switch things up as this change will likely bring positive benefits to your life.

農曆十月

(November 7th - December 6th) 癸亥
Be more prudent in your actions this month. Plan ahead and make sure you cover all the loopholes. Risks will only lead you to dangerous paths from which unexpected issues may lie.

農曆十一月

(December 7th 2018 - January 4th 2019) 甲子
You will find yourself spending more time at work while your relationships suffer from neglect. Do not let your loved ones feel shunned and instead work to strike a healthy balance between both aspects of your life.

農曆十二月

(January 5th - February 3rd 2019) 乙丑
You may experience some stomach issues this month such as stomach flu or other digestive issues. As such, you should pay attention to what you eat so that you can avoid the problem.

戊戌 Wu Xu Day

Overview

This is an important year for you to make great progress in your career. You will need to be confident enough to take some bold steps towards your goals. That being said, there may be some unforeseen hindrances ahead as a result of vile rumours and slander spread by individuals who do not want to see you succeed.

Wealth

While your financial outlook is positive, you will need to remain cautious if you are in a business partnership. Be aggressive in pursuing your goals and you will find it more rewarding than being passive. You can enjoy a great deal of wealth if you are strategic and prepared.

Relationships

Single men will have better Peach Blossom Luck than women. If you are in a steady relationship, this is a good year to get married. However, be careful if you are already married as there is a risk of extra-marital affairs.

Health

You need not worry about your health this month if you were born in the winter or spring months. If you were born in the autumn or summer, watch out head and limb injuries and be wary of any possible growths or tumours. Make sure you see the doctor at the first sign of trouble.

Career

Career advancement is possible for you, provided you have put in the work. Procrastination or being too passive may cause you to miss out on great opportunities. As such, you must stay focused, determined, and always be ready to make the most of a situation.

農曆正月

(February 4th - March 4th) 甲寅
Spring babies may find themselves losing out to rivals this month. You will need to be more forceful and confident with your abilities in order to not get left behind.

農曆二月

(March 5th - April 4th) 乙卯
Support will be available for you this month. Your desire to do things differently will be met with help from your friends and family.

農曆三月

(April 5th - May 4th) 丙辰
This is an auspicious month for you. As such, consider working in a team so that you can share this prosperity with others and in turn gain more. Invest your earnings in a wisely to maximise profits.

農曆四月

(May 5th - June 5th) 丁巳
This is a potentially difficult month as you fall into tense situations with those close to you over money. However, you should stay calm or risk worsening the situation.

農曆五月

(June 6th - July 6th) 戊午
You may receive some good news this month especially in terms of your career, which may mean a career advancement of some sort.

農曆六月

(July 7th - August 6th) 己未
This is not a good month for you to remain in your comfort zone and perpetuate rigidity and a lack of compromise. Strive to be more adaptable, as this will enable you to resolve problems easier.

農曆七月

(August 7th - September 7th) 庚申
Married couples should avoid arguments this month for the benefit of all. Drivers need to be extra careful on the road as accidents are likely, with your right leg being particularly vulnerable.

農曆八月

(September 8th - October 7th) 辛酉
You will be blessed with great ideas this month, so do not hesitate to seize the opportunity to turn your ideas into a reality and get going with your projects.

農曆九月

(October 8th - November 6th) 壬戌
This is a good month for teamwork, as other people's ideas will inspire you and lead to creativity among all.

農曆十月

(November 7th - December 6th) 癸亥
Avoid making any solid decisions this month if you are in the midst of pursuing a partnership, though you can think over your plans and prepare in the meantime.

農曆十一月

(December 7th 2018 - January 4th 2019) 甲子
You will find yourself lavished with attention and praise from others this month thanks to the excellent ideas you have shared with others. Do not hold back from claiming the credit you deserve.

農曆十二月

(January 5th - February 3rd 2019) 乙丑
You are vulnerable to bodily injuries this month. While the injuries will not be too serious, you should still be careful with your limbs in particular.

己亥 Ji Hai Day

己
Ji
亥
Hai

Overview
This is a crucial year for your career to grow and get to a place you want it to be. There may be some unforeseen hindrances along the way as a result of gossip and rumours spread by unkind individuals who do not want to see you succeed. You need only be mentally prepared for this and know how to focus on the work at hand instead of getting caught up with these trivialities. Form a strong network of trusted individuals who can help you achieve your goals.

Wealth
If you were born during the spring or summer, a collaboration, joint venture or partnership will be greatly beneficial to you. You will need to work hard to form these relationships and establish a strong network. Remember to also take the time and effort to be creative so that you may come up with new ideas that can turn the tide of your progress for the better.

Relationships
Your relationships may be less smooth-sailing than you hope for as there is potential competition lurking. You will have to step up your efforts to retain your interests and watch out for external disturbances. Those in relationships should remember to keep their integrity.

Health
While you will enjoy good health this year, keep an eye out of your blood pressure and diet. Also try to control your stress and anxiety as this could cause you to fall ill. Additionally, watch out for eye-related problems and skin allergies.

Career
Engage in teamwork this year as it will help you move forward in your career. Also make sure you keep your emotions in check otherwise you will jeopardize potential promotions coming your way. Meanwhile, entrepreneurs will face particular difficulties. Maintaining your composure will help you make better decisions throughout the year.

農曆正月

(February 4th - March 4th) 甲寅
Do not be too easy going to the point that you let opportunities pass you by, lest you miss out on precious opportunities.

農曆二月

(March 5th - April 4th) 乙卯
Do not shy away from sharing your ideas with others as it may lead to stagnancy in your work. There will be the time for you to retreat, but this is not it.

農曆三月

(April 5th - May 4th) 丙辰
You will need to be perseverant, energetic and determined in order to snag a possible promotion this month. Do not give up too easily and it will be worth it.

農曆四月

(May 5th - June 5th) 丁巳
You will experience some complications in your romantic life this month, but you should not take them to the workplace and let it affect your work.

農曆五月

(June 6th - July 6th) 戊午
You may have to lend some money to someone close to you this month. You will also need to be more watchful over your business accounts, especially if you have a partner.

農曆六月

(July 7th - August 6th) 己未
A friend may be a surprise source of interesting new insights or information this month. However, do not exploit them or abuse your connection to them.

農曆七月

(August 7th - September 7th) 庚申
This may be a month of emotional turmoil for you this month. As such, make sure to keep your temper in check and think carefully before making a decision.

農曆八月

(September 8th - October 7th) 辛酉
If you travel northwards this month, make sure you watch what you eat as there is a chance of food poisoning if you are not careful.

農曆九月

(October 8th - November 6th) 壬戌
Trying new things will bring you great benefits this month. Do not be afraid to take the leap and innovate fresh ideas.

農曆十月

(November 7th - December 6th) 癸亥
Keep your arrogance in check this month as there is a chance it will lead to bad decisions. Do not let your emotions drive you until you have cleared your head.

農曆十一月

(December 7th 2018 - January 4th 2019) 甲子
You will do well to engage in teamwork this month, as sharing the burden with others will ease your job and bring rewards. This will be especially true if you were born during the summer.

農曆十二月

(January 5th - February 3rd 2019) 乙丑
Workplace obligations do not mean you should neglect your relationships. It is not right to neglect your loved ones for the sake of temporary satisfaction.

庚子 **Geng Zi Day**

Overview

This year brings tidings of a major life event or decision. You may have to deal with radical and abrupt change. Take this as an opportunity to break out of your comfort zone and move ahead. Such pursuits are blessed, with the signs pointing to a favourable outcome. Be bold enough to change up your methods in order to progress with your efforts this year.

Wealth

Your wealth pursuits may not be immediately rewarded this year, though that does not mean you should give up. Take this downtime to plan for the future and lay out solid plans. Setting the foundation and planning contingencies will greatly benefit you.

Relationships

You may have to work harder at managing your relationships. Men in particular will need to spend more time nurturing your relationship as it is likely you have been neglecting your partner. Women may have the chance to find love at the workplace, though keep in mind it will not last and as such it might be best to just focus on your career.

Health

If you were born during the autumn and winter, you may be bothered by frequent bouts of stomach flu and digestive problems this year. Otherwise, you are likely to be in pretty good health. Nevertheless, take this time to make improvements to your diet.

Career

Overall, your work will go smoothly despite occasional conflicts with your superiors due to differences in personalities. You may want to explain yourself in writing as it likely to be a clearer medium rather than speech.

農曆正月

(February 4th - March 4th) 甲寅
There may be troubles on the home front. Do not spend too much time thinking about it as this will cause you to lose focus.

農曆二月

(March 5th - April 4th) 乙卯
This is a good month for you to turn to your team and see what they can help you with.

農曆三月

(April 5th - May 4th) 丙辰
Some of your work may be held back this month, but that does not mean you should slow down and give up the grind.

農曆四月

(May 5th - June 5th) 丁巳
You should exercise more control over your words this month, as there is a chance your possible insensitivity will cause offence to others.

農曆五月

(June 6th - July 6th) 戊午
You may experience possible financial windfalls this month. Think about sharing your rewards with others as they too have played a part in your success.

農曆六月

(July 7th - August 6th) 己未
Do not be afraid to let your more aggressive side come out this month, especially if you want to be able to see some results in terms of wealth.

農曆七月

(August 7th - September 7th) 庚申
There is a possibility that you embark on some travels this month. As such, you will need to be more careful on the road as there is a possibility of accidents.

農曆八月

(September 8th - October 7th) 辛酉
Do not be too prideful to ask for help at work. There will be Noble People around you who are willing and capable.

農曆九月

(October 8th - November 6th) 壬戌
You will be more inspired and motivated this month to come up with creative, new ideas.

農曆十月

(November 7th - December 6th) 癸亥
You will need to be more careful with your money or other personal items this month as there is a risk of losing them. There is also the likelihood of an unplanned expenditure due to medical bills.

農曆十一月

(December 7th 2018 - January 4th 2019) 甲子
You may attract more petty folk this month who spread rumours and gossip. Distance yourself your them as best you can.

農曆十二月

(January 5th - February 3rd 2019) 乙丑
Those born during the autumn or winter may find that collaboration and teamwork will bring the best results this month.

辛丑 Xin Chou Day

Overview

This may prove to be a challenging year as sudden changes may come into your life. You will be confused by the uncertainty and be driven to be more proactive in your response to these changes. You will only gain favourable outcomes if you seek out opportunities, especially in terms of your wealth. While this may consume much of your time and energy, if you stay focussed, your hard work will pay off.

Wealth

You will need to work a lot harder to make money this year. You may be required to create opportunities for yourself and renew old approaches or projects. Seek out other people for fresh ideas on how you can innovate. Collaboration will bring you much benefit and help you cultivate your financial position.

Relationships

Men will possess better Peach Blossom Luck, but they will still need to put in effort to see some improvement in their love lives. It will be beneficial for you to enlist help of your friends to acquaint you with some suitable candidates. Single women will need to be more independent in looking for a partner. They will have more luck seeking romance during their travels.

Health

Pay more attention to your health this year, especially during the latter half of the year, as you are in a weaker state than usual. You should work at improving your immune system by adopting a healthy diet and regular exercise. Your legs will also be prone to injuries, so do be careful when you are involved in strenuous physical activities.

Career

Be more creative with your work this year and you find that you start having an edge over others. Strategize well by keeping a few contingency plans in your pocket so that you are well-prepared to deal with loopholes or sudden challenges at work. Change is the main theme of the situation at work this year.

農曆正月

(February 4th - March 4th) 甲寅
Competition heats up at the workplace this month and you will need to stay on top of your work so others do not get the better of you.

農曆二月

(March 5th - April 4th) 乙卯
This month brings poorer career luck as it will not bode well for you to try closing business deals or attend important meetings as they will not yield positive results.

農曆三月

(April 5th - May 4th) 丙辰
You should try coming up with new strategies and ideas this month as innovation will be the way you get ahead of the curve and establish a fresh start.

農曆四月

(May 5th - June 5th) 丁巳
This is a good month for you to embark on some travelling, as it can help inspire you get your creative juices flowing for new ideas. Be on the lookout of potential illnesses while on your travels.

農曆五月

(June 6th - July 6th) 戊午
This is a good month for you to try earning some extra wealth on the side. However, those born in the spring or summer may find themselves prone emotional volatility.

農曆六月

(July 7th - August 6th) 己未
Men will find this to be a challenging month, particularly in terms of their relationship. Arguments are frequent and may cause serious stress. Try to control your emotions so that the situation does not worsen beyond repair.

農曆七月

(August 7th - September 7th) 庚申
Those born in the winter or autumn will find themselves most prone to health problems this month. Despite this, they will experience strong Wealth Luck.

農曆八月

(September 8th - October 7th) 辛酉
Traveling in the southern hemisphere will bode well for your wealth and health this month. You will find that the holiday reinvigorates your spirit and ideas.

農曆九月

(October 8th - November 6th) 壬戌
You will have a surge of fresh ideas this month that you will be able to share with others at work.

農曆十月

(November 7th - December 6th) 癸亥
This is a good month for rest and rejuvenation. You should be giving yourself some time off to recuperate and bring your mental well-being back up.

農曆十一月

(December 7th 2018 - January 4th 2019) 甲子
Competition surges at the workplace, demanding harder work from you. Do not try to cheat your way out of this by using dirty tactics or shortcuts. Trying to undermine others by speaking ill of them will only come back to bite you.

農曆十二月

(January 5th - February 3rd 2019) 乙丑
You will find yourself to be the subject of malicious gossip this month. Ignore these trivialities and take it as a sign that you are doing better than most people.

壬寅 Ren Yin Day

Overview

Getting into partnerships and joint venture opportunities this year will yield great rewards for you. As an employee, you can also gain maximum benefits by co-operating with your colleagues and teaming up to finish your tasks. This does not mean you have to sacrifice your independence, though to ensure a smooth sailing year, you are recommended to collaborate with others as often as you can.

Wealth

Wealth opportunities will arise from your social network through mutual friends and extended contacts. Be sure to listen to the advice and opinions of others as they can become an important part of your pursuit of new opportunities.

Relationships

You find that your friends are connected to somebody you are attracted to. If you are in a relationship, work harder to maintain your commitment as there are potential instabilities ahead. Potential discrepancies could upset the bond of trust in your relationship.

Health

You will enjoy good health this year. However, those above thirty years of age must be mindful of their sugar intake as there is a risk of your cholesterol levels spiking. Go for medical check-ups as often as possible to ensure there are no problems with your blood sugar.

Career

Sociable individuals will find that their knack for making friends brings them great benefit this year. Those who are more introverted will still benefit from connecting with existing social circles regularly. However, there is a chance you will have to deal with gossip and rumours, so be careful of who you trust with sensitive information.

農曆正月

(February 4th - March 4th) 甲寅
Do not be discouraged by apparent favouritism in the office. Be the more mature individual by moving ahead and continuing to do your job. Lend your support to others and be open to their ideas so that you will eventually come to be seen as a valuable part of the workplace.

農曆二月

(March 5th - April 4th) 乙卯
You are in need of an outlet at which you can share your ideas openly. Make sure to seek out individuals who are willing to listen.

農曆三月

(April 5th - May 4th) 丙辰
Arguments with colleagues and partners may plague your work life this month but do keep a firm hold over your temper so that things do not escalate.

農曆四月

(May 5th - June 5th) 丁巳
You will be rewarded with extra wealth as a result of your hard work and commitment. However, be careful with your spending lest you waste all that you have been given.

農曆五月

(June 6th - July 6th) 戊午
Your escalating stress is causing your immune system to falter. Make sure you get enough rest to move away from the stress of your life to prevent illness from taking hold.

農曆六月

(July 7th - August 6th) 己未
Be careful with your words and actions this month, especially with sarcasm. Think of how you might accidentally hurt others if you are not more sensitive.

農曆七月

(August 7th - September 7th) 庚申
You will experience much Wealth Luck this month, especially if you were born in the summer.

農曆八月

(September 8th - October 7th) 辛酉
There is a chance that you may sent to travel for work this month. Make the most of this opportunity by embracing it fully and being open minded.

農曆九月

(October 8th - November 6th) 壬戌
You may be feeling unhappy or unsatisfied with a certain someone in your life this month. Sort things out with that person by communicating clearly and honestly.

農曆十月

(November 7th - December 6th) 癸亥
Your friends and colleagues may pose a distraction this month. Stay focused instead of indulging in idle, wasteful activities.

農曆十一月

(December 7th 2018 - January 4th 2019) 甲子
Travel to the south may bring great career advancements for you this month.

農曆十二月

(January 5th - February 3rd 2019) 乙丑
People around you will be able to inspire you and bring out some good ideas, so make sure you open yourself up to people and receive their ideas with gratefulness.

癸卯 **Gui Mao Day**

Overview

You will need to cultivate a habit of planning very meticulously. Good organisation skills will make the difference in whether you succeed or not. Take a more structured approach to your endeavours and avoid reckless decisions. In any case, you will need to be prepared for the coming negotiations with prospective collaborators that will ultimately lead to a future partnership.

Wealth

Your wealth prospects this year are average. You will need to work very hard to make a breakthrough. However, your hard work will yield other results by solidifying strong foundations for the growth of your wealth in the future. However, this will only work if you are organised and plan well for the long term.

Relationships

Single men more likely to meet their future life partner this year. However, keep a low profile at first as your fledgling relationship may come under threat from outside forces. Single women should wait for spring to make their move, as it will be more auspicious for romance then.

Health

Your health is similarly average, especially if you were born in the autumn or winter. Stomach-related issues will crop up such as haemorrhoids and constipation. Take your symptoms seriously and make a visit to the doctor as soon as possible.

Career

You may be able to achieve extraordinary success in your career this year if you are willing to tough it out with an extremely busy schedule that may leave you exhausted. There will be a large number of responsibilities that come without reward at first, but your perseverance will be rewarded.

農曆正月

(February 4th - March 4th) 甲寅
You will find yourself rather jaded with your life this month especially if you are still living with your family.

農曆二月

(March 5th - April 4th) 乙卯
You will find yourself plagued by overthinking this month. You will have to get a grip on reality and start acting.

農曆三月

(April 5th - May 4th) 丙辰
There may be an outsider trying to meddle with your work or your home life this month. Ignore their presence and instead focus on your own tasks.

農曆四月

(May 5th - June 5th) 丁巳
Those who are married may find that arguments with their spouse are rather frequent this month. They should try their best to minimise these disagreements.

農曆五月

(June 6th - July 6th) 戊午
Opportunities will pass you by if you wait too long without acting. This is not a good time to be indecisive and hesitant. Work hard to chase your goals.

農曆六月

(July 7th - August 6th) 己未
Work at being more open and honest with others this month. If you keep things to yourself, you will end up wallowing alone.

農曆七月

(August 7th - September 7th) 庚申
Check yourself that your greed does not get out of hand this month, or else you may be easily tempted into doing something unethical for money.

農曆八月

(September 8th - October 7th) 辛酉
Do not be hasty with your decisions this month in the hopes of quickly getting things out of the way. It is preferable that you postpone the decisions if you are unsure, rather than to go on impulse.

農曆九月

(October 8th - November 6th) 壬戌
A career advancement in the form of a promotion may come your way this month. Make sure all your work is settled properly and that you remain responsible over your tasks.

農曆十月

(November 7th - December 6th) 癸亥
Travelling to the south or east will bring you good luck this month.

農曆十一月

(December 7th 2018 - January 4th 2019) 甲子
Do not be easily fooled by deals that seem too good to be true this month. There is a chance that you may be taken advantage of.

農曆十二月

(January 5th - February 3rd 2019) 乙丑
You will need to be discerning about who you share your ideas with this month, as there are people out there who are looking to take credit for your work.

甲辰 Jia Chen Day

Overview
You will have to learn to come out stronger this year. You will need to have your focus and diligence at their highest capacity for you to be able to confront the unforeseen challenges ahead. The nature of the obstacles will also demand quick reactions, leaving no room for procrastination or hesitation. As such, avoid dividing your attention between too many things as this could negatively affect your focus and thus make it more difficult for you to succeed.

 ## Wealth
Your financial growth will depend on your proactivity and good decisions. Do not squander your opportunities by hesitate or putting others before yourself. This does not mean you should take advantage of others to reach your objectives, but you should be able to be aggressive in your favour and not be afraid to compete with your peers.

 ## Relationships
You will find it difficult to deal with your family members, particularly your mother and your potential significant other. You will need to be diplomatic and cautious when resolving these issues. If you are a man in a relationship, you will likely have to face the trials that come with having a girlfriend whose professional status and social network are overtaking yours.

 ## Health
You are likely to suffer injuries to your legs this year even though you will be in good physical health. Your eyes and stomach may also give you additional trouble. Rethink your diet and start fresh in order to curb any potential gastrointestinal issues this year.

Career
You will find that your learning speed is your strongest ability this year, and as such you should try to learn something new or gain a new skill. Be industrious with your opportunities and maintain a sense of momentum so that you continue to improve.

農曆正月

(February 4th - March 4th) 甲寅
You may find yourself running into trouble with the law this month especially if you are going to be driving a lot. As such, take care not to break any rules.

農曆二月

(March 5th - April 4th) 乙卯
You may achieve wealth this month if you put in the required time and effort. Do not expect riches to be simply bequeathed to you.

農曆三月

(April 5th - May 4th) 丙辰
Nothing will come of you trying to gain recognition at work this month. Instead, focus on working harder to gain more benefits in the long run.

農曆四月

(May 5th - June 5th) 丁巳
Competition escalates this month and as such, you will need to work hard to not be left behind.

農曆五月

(June 6th - July 6th) 戊午
Despite not receiving affirmation from your boss this month, you still need to see the silver lining and find the learning experience in this situation.

農曆六月

(July 7th - August 6th) 己未
You will need to do your best to stay energized this month, as there are many demotivating and tiring influences around you that may impede you from finishing your tasks.

農曆七月

(August 7th - September 7th) 庚申
There is a strong likelihood that you will go travelling this month, but you will need to watch what you eat as there is a risk of food poisoning.

農曆八月

(September 8th - October 7th) 辛酉
Rivalry is strong at the workplace this month, but you will need to make sure you remain diplomatic despite this.

農曆九月

(October 8th - November 6th) 壬戌
Those born during the autumn are likely to experience a good month this time, with the possibility of a pay rise or promotion.

農曆十月

(November 7th - December 6th) 癸亥
This is a good month in general for you to take on financial endeavours. Married men should be careful against possible instanced of extra-marital dalliances.

農曆十一月

(December 7th 2018 - January 4th 2019) 甲子
Refrain from doing anything you might regret when it comes to the law as you will certainly pay the price for your transgressions.

農曆十二月

(January 5th - February 3rd 2019) 乙丑
You may find yourself attacked by petty gossip this month. As such, avoid groups that dabble in such activities and focus on your own tasks.

六十甲子 Forecast for 2018 based on Day of Birth

乙巳 Yi Si Day

Overview

You will enjoy a greatly auspicious year especially in terms of wealth opportunities. You will not need to worry too much when making decisions for your business as this is your time to thrive and pursue new opportunities. Even the most spontaneous actions will yield great results for you. Take this year as a good way to launch yourself forward and give yourself a head start in life.

 ## Wealth

Those born in the spring months will have especially good luck in gaining capital. Optimise your chances by making sure that you are on the alert for all the opportunities that come your way. Too much hesitation will only rob you of your momentum and cause you to miss out on important opportunities.

 ## Relationships

If you are a man in a long-term relationship, this year is a good time to consider settling down. Married men need to work on not prioritizing other aspects of their life over their relationship. You will need to spend time nurturing your marriage or it will be too late.

 ## Health

Your well-being may decline this year especially if you were born during the summer or autumn. Make sure you prioritize your health and look after it accordingly, taking care not to take it for granted in your pursuit of more temporary pleasures.

 ## Career

You will likely be blessed with a promotion this year, as your efforts at work are finally recognised. Along with this is also the possibility of a salary increment, and a boost of your reputation at work.

農曆正月

(February 4th - March 4th) 甲寅

This is a good month to initiate teamwork at the workplace with your peers. Share your challenges and rewards with them, and you will find work to be a more rewarding experience.

農曆二月

(March 5th - April 4th) 乙卯

This is an auspicious time for you to take on new challenges and projects at work. This will work out in your favour especially if you were born in the spring.

農曆三月

(April 5th - May 4th) 丙辰

Those born in the spring or winter will enjoy good Wealth Luck this month. However, the opposite is true for those born in the summer or autumn.

農曆四月

(May 5th - June 5th) 丁巳

A career advancement is coming your way, either in the form of a pay raise or a promotion. That being said, you must first prove that you deserve this opportunity by working hard for it.

農曆五月

(June 6th - July 6th) 戊午

There will be changes at the workplace this month, most likely in the form of new superiors. They will bring with them a new of doing things and revive the atmosphere at work.

農曆六月

(July 7th - August 6th) 己未

Tension is building at the workplace especially for those born in the summer or autumn. Tread carefully so you do not get into too many arguments.

農曆七月

(August 7th - September 7th) 庚申

You will still need to watch your temper this month as you are prone to arguments. Be careful on the road so that such distractions do not cause you harm.

農曆八月

(September 8th - October 7th) 辛酉

You may find yourself laden with more burdens. Take some time off to step back and look at your responsibilities with fresh eyes, so that you may think of other ways to tackle them.

農曆九月

(October 8th - November 6th) 壬戌

This is not a month for you to get away with carelessness. If you are not more prudent, you will find yourself wasting much time on cleaning up your own mess.

農曆十月

(November 7th - December 6th) 癸亥

Do not be too quick in your judgment of others as you may miss out the deeper layers to their personality. There may be some colleagues who are using you, despite their appearance of kindness.

農曆十一月

(December 7th 2018 - January 4th 2019) 甲子

You may find yourself having to spend quite a lot of money this month. This in unavoidable as this is likely the result of having to spend on elderly members in your family.

農曆十二月

(January 5th - February 3rd 2019) 乙丑

You are beginning to feel that you are being taken advantage of at the workplace amongst a team of people who rely on you to pull their weight. You should be honest with your feelings and try to find to find a solution to this problem.

丙午 **Bing Wu Day**

Overview

You will enjoy and overwhelmingly positive year. All the hard work you invested will pay off and make your dreams a reality. Leap at the chance to seize opportunities as they come your way. Your wealth luck is promising, and as such you need to make sure that you are capitalising on all your options so that you open up more avenues for progress.

 Wealth

Opportunities to accumulate wealth are abundant this year, requiring proactivity on your part to make the most of them. If you are in a partnership, exercise caution as there is a possibility of disagreements over finances. Do not let this escalate out of control.

 Relationships

Married men need to commit to be faithful in their marriage, as there is a temptation to be involved in an extra-marital affair that will bring about the fall of your marriage. Remember your duties and obligations and always choose the high road. Individuals who have not taken the next step may find that this is a good year to do so.

 Health

Those born in autumn and summer will have moderate health this year. It is important to take extra precautions with your physical well-being as there is a possibility of headaches and migraines.

 Career

Those born during the spring can expect a career advancement or promotion. That being said, this will not be handed to you and you will need to actually put in the right effort. Keep up your good work and you will see better results.

農曆正月

(February 4th - March 4th) 甲寅
Do not be afraid to cut people off if they have demonstrated a lack of commitment to your relationship. In terms of health, you will need to be mindful of your head as it may be prone to injury.

農曆二月

(March 5th - April 4th) 乙卯
Your colleagues may be pressuring you into making a difficult decision. Do not give in for the sake of making them go away.

農曆三月

(April 5th - May 4th) 丙辰
You may be rewarded by a surprise financial windfall this month as a result of your hard work in recent times. As such, do not worry about taking some time off as you have earned it.

農曆四月

(May 5th - June 5th) 丁巳
Be more careful with your work so that you do not present your superiors with unacceptable work. Try to be more thorough so as to avoid their disappointment and chastisement.

農曆五月

(June 6th - July 6th) 戊午
There is a possibility that old legal issues will come back and demand to be settled once and for all. Be careful so as to not get into more trouble, for instance by making sure you pay your loans and fines on time.

農曆六月

(July 7th - August 6th) 己未
You may experience some issues with your stomach this month and as such you will need to think about a better diet. Avoid anything of dubious hygiene to stay safe.

農曆七月

(August 7th - September 7th) 庚申
You may experience some health problems especially relating to your head. This may be due to carelessness on your part where let yourself get distracted and accidentally hurt yourself. Those born in the summer may have leg injuries.

農曆八月

(September 8th - October 7th) 辛酉
You may need to go through some additional training at work so that you can learn more skills to deal with a new project this month.

農曆九月

(October 8th - November 6th) 壬戌
You may find yourself butting heads with certain colleagues this month as challenge and annoy you. Do not let yourself be pushed around and try to be more careful with who you trust.

農曆十月

(November 7th - December 6th) 癸亥
You may experience some problems with your eyes this month. Go see a doctor to diagnose the problem as soon as possible so that you know what you are dealing with.

農曆十一月

(December 7th 2018 - January 4th 2019) 甲子
You may find yourself embarking on some travelling this month. In doing so, you should continue to watch your expenses and be very careful not to overindulge. Also make sure you watch our for your possessions and personal documents.

農曆十二月

(January 5th - February 3rd 2019) 乙丑
Avoid procrastination as much as possible. Work on your tasks whenever you have time so as to make sure that you do not accumulate unnecessary workload later.

丁未 Ding Wei Day

Overview

This year, success can be yours if you persevere and do what is needed in order to move forward. There may be an opportunity to travel for work and it will most likely be beneficial to you. You can also use this chance to gain recognition for your work and build a reputation for yourself. Fight the tendency to get distracted and procrastinate, as it will be important for you to keep your eyes on the prize in order to garner results in your work.

 ## Wealth

Your finances this year are somewhat unstable. You should spend your savings on long-term investments rather than impulse purchases as your money is precious and should be used wisely to make the most of it. Exercise restraint and consolidate your finances whenever possible.

 ## Relationships

This will be a turbulent year for you if you are in a relationship. Married couples should sort out their problems as soon as possible to prevent them from escalating and possibly resulting in a separation or divorce. All in all, relationship issues will take up a big chunk of your time. It is vital that you find balance and not allow your personal problems to take over other aspects of your life.

 ## Health

You should be in good health this year aside from issues relating to your blood pressure and stomach. Change your diet and consider going for a thorough medical check-up. Watch your weight as the latter could cause serious health complications in the future.

 ## Career

Do your best to keep the momentum of your ideas and creativity flowing. Whenever an opportunity to travel arises, you should take it as it will be favourable for your career. Resist the urge to procrastinate and instead work to keep yourself occupied in order to avoid stagnation. This will help propel you towards success with your goals.

農曆正月

(February 4th - March 4th) 甲寅
This month may start off well for you in terms of wealth opportunities, which could see you make a good amount of profits.

農曆二月

(March 5th - April 4th) 乙卯
Networking can bring you great opportunities for success this month, as you will be able to meet people who can push you in the right direction and give you advice.

農曆三月

(April 5th - May 4th) 丙辰
A promotion is the works for you this month, especially if you were born in the autumn or winter. Do not waste time on your decisions or you may squander your opportunity.

農曆四月

(May 5th - June 5th) 丁巳
Do not allow your impulses and emotions to build to a boiling point this month by minimising interactions that can cause outbursts on your part.

農曆五月

(June 6th - July 6th) 戊午
You will receive financial reward from people willing to pay for your skills and expertise this month.

農曆六月

(July 7th - August 6th) 己未
You may find your energy and immune system prone to quickly draining.

農曆七月

(August 7th - September 7th) 庚申
Despite support from your friends, it will still be up to you to finish your own work. As such, you will need to be focused and hardworking.

農曆八月

(September 8th - October 7th) 辛酉
This is a good month for romance as your Peach Blossom Luck is strong. Therefore, you should put yourself out there and be more open to meeting others.

農曆九月

(October 8th - November 6th) 壬戌
There may be changes happening at work which may not necessarily benefit you. However, you can still try to take them as a learning experience and concentrate on more important goals.

農曆十月

(November 7th - December 6th) 癸亥
This is a good month to engage in teamwork. In addition, travellers should try to head south.

農曆十一月

(December 7th 2018 - January 4th 2019) 甲子
Your food allergies are likely to cause some health issues this month. You will also be moody and prone to irritation, so try to lay low and take care of yourself.

農曆十二月

(January 5th - February 3rd 2019) 乙丑
Married couples may themselves dealing with arguments. Learn to compromise and be patient with one another to avoid the escalation of disagreements.

戊申 Wu Shen Day

Overview

You will find this to be a smooth-sailing year wherein your plans can be executed without much worry. As you go along, you will hone your confidence in your abilities. Additionally, you will be blessed with auspicious Wealth Luck which will bring financial security. Your income is likely to be stable and as such, it will be counterproductive for you to take part in any kind of risky financial activities such as speculative investments or gambling. You will need to make sure that you stay ahead of the curve by planning ahead and being prudent.

 ## Wealth

Your positive Wealth Luck will persist throughout the year, possibly bringing you a pay raise. If you have your own business or are an entrepreneur, you should consider taking your business to greater heights by turning your attentions overseas to see if you have the opportunity to start afresh there. There will certainly be many more interested parties there who can help you along.

 ## Relationships

If you are in a steady relationship, you may want to think about settling down. This is especially true if you are a man who has been attached for some time. On the other hand, single women may find that you have captivated a few interested suitors. However, married women will have to watch out for potential temptations away from your relationship as well as arguments over money.

 ## Health

Though you will be in good physical condition this year, you should not neglect your healthcare by taking things for granted. This means you should continue to pay attention to your diet and maintain your exercise regime in order to keep yourself in top form. By continually taking care of your body, you are safeguarding it against future attacks onto your health.

 ## Career

Your career prospects are promising this year, bringing with it the possibility of travel, which will have a positive effect on your career advancement plans. It is likely to bring rewards both in terms of your reputation and finances. Do not be afraid to explore this avenue as it will bring great rewards.

農曆正月

(February 4th - March 4th) 甲寅
This month you will have to avoid risky investments or business schemes as there is a possibility that you may be tricked you out of your money, especially if you are in a partnership or business.

農曆二月

(March 5th - April 4th) 乙卯
You will be facing intense competition and envy from others this month. That being said, this is only because your talent and creativity has created great impact and gained recognition.

農曆三月

(April 5th - May 4th) 丙辰
Your investments will begin to reap profits this month for you. However, refrain from making any further investments as the timing is not good for you and not yield the same results.

農曆四月

(May 5th - June 5th) 丁巳
This is a good month for you to consider new activities that can help you relax and stay calm such as yoga or meditation, which can help you manage your stress from work.

農曆五月

(June 6th - July 6th) 戊午
You may find yourself dealing with some health issues this month including injuries, particularly to your head. Migraines and headaches are also likely.

農曆六月

(July 7th - August 6th) 己未
Try to keep an open mind and be flexible this month. Otherwise, you may find yourself doing the same thing over and over and draining your resources.

農曆七月

(August 7th - September 7th) 庚申
Do not be afraid to be more assertive, focused and determined. This will bring more productivity and help you ignore distractions.

農曆八月

(September 8th - October 7th) 辛酉
You will find your emotions easily drained this month and as such, you should try to seek the support of friends and family or you may become overwhelmed by the pressure.

農曆九月

(October 8th - November 6th) 壬戌
You will need to keep your head down and focus on your work this month. Try not to get drawn into sticky situations as you need to stay focused.

農曆十月

(November 7th - December 6th) 癸亥
Be generous with the help that you offer others this month, especially your own family members. However, you still should not let others take advantage of you.

農曆十一月

(December 7th 2018 - January 4th 2019) 甲子
Do not give into the impulse to spend on your temptations this month. Do not fall for deceptive sales and promotions and keep your credit card on a lockdown.

農曆十二月

(January 5th - February 3rd 2019) 乙丑
Avoid investment schemes or business start-ups this month, as anything you undertake right now will not yield positive results.

己酉 Ji You Day

己 Ji
酉 You

Overview

You are blessed with a Moderate Luck this year, meaning that your experiences will be mostly positive. Most of your opportunities for wealth will come from travelling, where you have the opportunity to widen your networks and gain valuable experience in new markets. Those born during autumn or winter should be prioritizing their health this year.

 ## Wealth

Your financial endeavours are likely to pay off this year. Even investments made in the past will begin to bear fruit. At this time, do not let your work ethic drop as maintaining your productivity and momentum will greatly improve your reputation and even bring a pay rise. Business owners can consider expanding their business without fear of geographical limits.

 ## Relationships

Single men will experience positive Peach Blossom Luck this year. There is a chance that you will meet your significant other. Married men have to be wary, however, as minor flirtation with other parties can potentially lead to something more damaging to your marriage. Single women will also enjoy good Peach Blossom Luck.

 ## Health

Those born during autumn or winter will need to focus on their health. There may be minor, though not insignificant issues surrounding your stomach and other gastrointestinal organs such as the liver. There is also a risk injuries to your limbs especially on the right side of your body.

 ## Career

Your career will experience significant advancements this year. Business travels will coincide with promotions, and even if you are thinking of changing jobs, there are likely to be no shortage of offers coming your way. However, make sure you think carefully before making any decisions.

農曆正月

(February 4th - March 4th) 甲寅
Competition rises at work this month. However, do not react to this by becoming a recluse. Teamwork with your colleagues will be essential to everyone's prosperity.

農曆二月

(March 5th - April 4th) 乙卯
Though you may experience some positive wealth luck this month, you may be distracted by some minor health issues. Make sure you deal with your health before worrying too much about money.

農曆三月

(April 5th - May 4th) 丙辰
Those born in the summer or autumn will have great luck collaborating with others for group projects and collaborative projects.

農曆四月

(May 5th - June 5th) 丁巳
Be more prudent with your spending and finances this month. Avoid short-term investment schemes that seem too good to be true, especially if you were born during the autumn.

農曆五月

(June 6th - July 6th) 戊午
You may the lucky recipient of a job promotion this month. Take some time to celebrate, though you should try to get back to your responsibilities as soon as possible as much preparation will be needed.

農曆六月

(July 7th - August 6th) 己未
You will need to take care with your driving this month as there is a chance of accidents or entanglements with the law that may bring great trouble.

農曆七月

(August 7th - September 7th) 庚申
This is the good month for you to try new skills and go for new experiences that you have always wanted to be a part of.

農曆八月

(September 8th - October 7th) 辛酉
Single women should take this month of good Peach Blossom Luck to seek out romance. Do not be afraid to make the first move as this will bring good results.

農曆九月

(October 8th - November 6th) 壬戌
No man is an island. Better results at work can be achieved if you step out of your comfort zone and team up with your colleagues.

農曆十月

(November 7th - December 6th) 癸亥
Emotions run high this month, making you prone to involvement in arguments this month. Do not let your pride and ego get in the way of compromise between you and the other party.

農曆十一月

(December 7th 2018 - January 4th 2019) 甲子
Be careful that your plans do not have any loopholes and may possibly bring about the collapse of your project. Be flexible with changes and humble enough to accept criticism.

農曆十二月

(January 5th - February 3rd 2019) 乙丑
Married couples or those in relationships may find themselves facing off over monetary issues. Try to control your emotions so you do not let such fights go out of hand.

庚戌 Geng Xu Day

Overview

This year may bring some challenges into your life that can be solved with the help of those around you. Keep your social networks active so that it is easier for you to reach out to people you know have the experience and resources to help you. Additionally, this will probably not be a good year for you in terms of wealth, but you can always turn it around by using it a transition period in which you build solid plans for the future.

Wealth

There will be no extraordinary events in terms of your wealth as you avoid a financial roller coaster this year. That being said, you need to guard against reckless spending as such impulsive behaviour with your finances will be your undoing. If you feel the itch to spend, you should instead direct your money to investments or opportunities that will help you generate more wealth.

Relationships

This is not a strong year for your luck with romance either. If you are in a relationship, there is a chance of frequent disagreements that strain your relationship. If you are single, it is likely that you will remain so and as such you are better off focusing on other areas of your life outside of romance.

Health

Be mindful of your kidneys and blood pressure this year by going for regular check-ups and being vigilant with your diet and exercise. It will be wise for you to attend to any medical issues immediately instead of waiting and letting them fester. Skin problems and allergies are also a potential threat, especially if you were born during the summer.

Career

A career change may take place this year for you. As such, you will need to be adaptable and flexible so that you continue to thrive in your new environment. Forming partnerships will be highly beneficial, as it makes your endeavours far more efficient and secure, thus boosting your new career significantly.

農曆正月

(February 4th - March 4th) 甲寅
You will need to watch your temper this month and opt instead for more diplomatic methods of conflict resolution.

農曆二月

(March 5th - April 4th) 乙卯
There is possibility of increased competition at work this month. You need to make sure you are prepared to take on the challenge. There is also a risk of sore throats and fever.

農曆三月

(April 5th - May 4th) 丙辰
Languor may plague you this month, resulted in a lack of motivation. Do not get lazy and procrastinate your work as you will not be able to get any work done if you do not step it up.

農曆四月

(May 5th - June 5th) 丁巳
Your friends will always be available for you to seek out for advice and support. Be careful with your decisions and seek consultations with other people who will be able to help you make better decisions.

農曆五月

(June 6th - July 6th) 戊午
You may need additional funding for a project. Do not be afraid to ask for assistance. You should be as prepared for this scenario as possible and plan your strategies.

農曆六月

(July 7th - August 6th) 己未
There is a chance for you to reap better financial gains at work this month.

農曆七月

(August 7th - September 7th) 庚申
Many new opportunities for financial gain will come your way this month along with more authority and power. This will not be handed to you as you will need to work hard first to acquire the trust and respect of others.

農曆八月

(September 8th - October 7th) 辛酉
Do not give in to rashness just because you are impatient. Impulsiveness at this time will not do you any good as it may result in you taking shortcuts that greatly harm your endeavours. Resist the temptation to take the easy way out and instead resolve to work hard and be patient with your results.

農曆九月

(October 8th - November 6th) 壬戌
You will find yourself coming up with new creative ideas this month that have the potential to become something real. However, these ideas will remain fantasies if you do not put in the required work.

農曆十月

(November 7th - December 6th) 癸亥
Your talents and hard work will finally be noticed this month by those who are in charge. They will reward you with praise and you will become revered for the work that you have done.

農曆十一月

(December 7th 2018 - January 4th 2019) 甲子
You may come into many arguments with your significant other this month which are at constant risk of toppling over into destructive territory. Always try taking the high road and conceding over compromising. It is important for you to work on repairing the fractures rather than allow them to deepen.

農曆十二月

(January 5th - February 3rd 2019) 乙丑
Resist the urge to use your tongue bitingly this month. Every now and then, you may want to launch a sarcastic or harsh remark, but this will only result in offence and hurt on the side of the other party.

辛亥 Xin Hai Day

Xin

Hai

Overview

This year, you will need to work to gain the success you desire and pay special attention to work that requires rigid plans and strict deadlines. Aside from that, you may be getting an assignment in a foreign land, which you should accept. Make sure you behave diplomatically and professionally so that you maintain a good reputation everywhere you go. Students can also look forward to getting good results in their examinations.

 Wealth

Be mindful of your spending habits this year as there is a chance that you will overspend. Material possessions will not bring true happiness if they ultimately only bring financial detriment. You must exercise discipline in your spending and if you want to make any investments, you should opt for the more short-term and risk-free options.

 Relationships

You should try to prevent your friends from interfering in your love life as their actions will only serve to further exacerbate any rifts between you and your partner. That being said, women will have better luck with their relationships. Married couples should trust their own instincts and not listen to what others say or give in to unfounded suspicions.

 Health

Your health will be average at best this year. You may experience some trouble with your ears and as such you should see a doctor the moment you feel something is amiss. Your blood pressure may also be an issue especially if you are in your mid-thirties or older. Be on the lookout for any symptoms and seek help immediately.

Career

If you work with education, you will have a fruitful year so be prepared to work hard for your career advancement. If you are in a different industry, you will need to do some forward planning if you want to succeed. Watch your words around others so as to avoid offending them. Always think before you speak and do not let yourself be carried away by your emotions.

農曆正月

(February 4th - March 4th) 甲寅
This is a good month for your Wealth Luck, and as such you will need to be proactive in seeking out opportunities to generate more profits.

農曆二月

(March 5th - April 4th) 乙卯
People who were born during the summer will find themselves dealing with some minor illnesses this month, such as fevers or sore throats.

農曆三月

(April 5th - May 4th) 丙辰
People who were born during the winter can expect more success coming their way at the workplace in the form of a career advancement.

農曆四月

(May 5th - June 5th) 丁巳
You may feel yourself being overwhelmed by workplace burdens this month, but you can get through it if you work at your own pace.

農曆五月

(June 6th - July 6th) 戊午
You will find yourself coming up with new ideas this month that will be able to help you garner some side income.

農曆六月

(July 7th - August 6th) 己未
You will have a busy month ahead, but you will be able to pull through if collaborate with your teammates.

農曆七月

(August 7th - September 7th) 庚申
You will need to tread carefully around others and scrutinise your offers carefully. There is a risk that some people are out there trying to steal your ideas.

農曆八月

(September 8th - October 7th) 辛酉
Pregnant women should be more careful with their safety this month while everyone else should be mindful of potential injuries to the right limb.

農曆九月

(October 8th - November 6th) 壬戌
You may be inspired to change things up in your life this month, and as such, you should seize whatever opportunities come your war and quickly make plans.

農曆十月

(November 7th - December 6th) 癸亥
It will be important to avoid risky endeavours this month. You should instead plan ahead and focus on the details which will help you deal with potential fallouts in the future.

農曆十一月

(December 7th 2018 - January 4th 2019) 甲子
Work may be taking up most of your time but you should not neglect your loved ones as they deserve some care from you as well.

農曆十二月

(January 5th - February 3rd 2019) 乙丑
You may have some health issues to look after this month related to your stomach or digestive problems. Therefore, you will need to be more mindful of what you eat.

壬子 Ren Zi Day

Overview

You may find yourself dealing with stagnation this year especially when it comes to your career. This may be due to the fact that you have not been strategic in who you work with, sometimes teaming up with people who do not carry their weight and use you to get ahead. As such, it is best for you to strive for foreign assignments and keep yourself busy.

 ## Wealth

Your wealth prospects can be enhanced if you seek out assignments overseas. If you own a business, success can be yours if you enter into a partnership with others or expand your business towards the north. However, be careful with your spending and focus instead on saving up.

 ## Relationships

Couples will find that this is a tumultuous year for relationships. You will begin to have feelings of neglect and resentment as a result of feeling used. You will need to be honest with your spouse about these issues. If you are single, you are advised to remain so, as a relationship this year will be too troublesome.

 ## Health

You are at high risk of gaining a great deal of weight and suffering from high blood cholesterol this year. As such, you will need to monitor your diet, especially the amount of sugar you consume. Do not be afraid to make long-term changes for your own benefit.

 ## Career

Travel is the way to go this year. You are in much need of fresh perspectives and new ideas. You may also want to consider transferring to another department or moving up to a higher position. This is because a challenging new work situation will lead to self-improvement and career advancement.

農曆正月

(February 4th - March 4th) 甲寅
You will be given new responsibilities at work from your boss. Team up with your colleagues to successfully tackle these tasks.

農曆二月

(March 5th - April 4th) 乙卯
Listen to and value the ideas of others as much as your own this month, as you may be surprised by how effective they end up being.

農曆三月

(April 5th - May 4th) 丙辰
Do not give in to procrastination this month, as this will only add to your problems and stress. Work hard at managing your time properly.

農曆四月

(May 5th - June 5th) 丁巳
You will be plagued by ailments to your stomach this month and as such, you should see a doctor as soon as symptoms occur.

農曆五月

(June 6th - July 6th) 戊午
Be wary of dishonest colleagues at the workplace who are trying to steal your ideas. Be more discerning about who you trust with such information.

農曆六月

(July 7th - August 6th) 己未
You may begin to feel stifled and unfulfilled in your career, leading to lethargy and frustration at the workplace. You will need to think on the positive side and adjust your attitude to avoid negative effects.

農曆七月

(August 7th - September 7th) 庚申
Your Wealth Luck is looking up this month and as such, you can be prepared to gain more rewards than usual.

農曆八月

(September 8th - October 7th) 辛酉
You will be desperately seeking some time for yourself this month. However, you will have many tasks to address which you should deal with immediately as procrastination will only make matters worse.

農曆九月

(October 8th - November 6th) 壬戌
Go ahead and seek out some down time in the form of a vacation to make up for all the stress you have been enduring.

農曆十月

(November 7th - December 6th) 癸亥
Your good luck with travelling will continue this month, and as such you should keep up the globe-trekking and seek out more experiences.

農曆十一月

(December 7th 2018 - January 4th 2019) 甲子
If you are in a partnership, you will need to be more careful regarding transparency and accountability. Keep an eye out for potential unethical behaviour that may be occurring behind your back.

農曆十二月

(January 5th - February 3rd 2019) 乙丑
This is the month for you to get in touch with your relationships and start paying more attention to your loved ones. Work at nurturing the trust and honesty you share with one another.

癸丑 Gui Chou Day

Gui

Chou

Overview
You will have the proper luck to build various kinds of professional connections this year. If you are a white-collar worker, you can expect to form stronger relations with your colleagues. On the other hand, business owners can look forward to collaborations, joint ventures or partnerships. It is crucial for you to realise that teamwork is the key to progress. Being more open-minded could open up many more opportunities for you.

 Wealth
This is an auspicious year for you in terms of your wealth. Be grateful to those who once assisted you financially or had a hand in your success. This is also a good time for you to go out and find suitable candidates to collaborate with you in your business.

 Relationships
It is advisable for you to concentrate on your career rather than try to look for relationships this year. While you will not be short of romantic candidates, you will always find yourself with the short end of the stick. If you are in a relationship, you will need to stay committed and not neglect those who are waiting for your affection.

 Health
Do not take your health for granted especially if you were born during the winter. It will be best that you get a full medical check-up to ensure that all is well. As your immune system will be somewhat weak, you may fall ill frequently and experience prolonged symptoms.

 Career
The best method for your career advancement this year is by collaborating with others. Therefore, you should be open to what others have to offer and make sure you listen to their ideas. If you are an employee, it is vital that you maintain a good impression in the eyes of your superiors as their support is crucial for your success.

農曆正月

(February 4th - March 4th) 甲寅
You will have a good month ahead of you this time where you can share your ideas with your superiors knowing that they will be supportive.

農曆二月

(March 5th - April 4th) 乙卯
This is the month for you to ensure that your superiors at work recognise your work and acknowledge your value in the workplace.

農曆三月

(April 5th - May 4th) 丙辰
Teamwork will bring you ahead, and as such you should make an effort to include others in your ventures and be open-minded to their ideas. Accord them the recognition they deserve as well.

農曆四月

(May 5th - June 5th) 丁巳
There may be some issues related to your stomach this month and as such you will need to be mindful of your diet.

農曆五月

(June 6th - July 6th) 戊午
Your mother's health will be an issue for you this month and could possibly result in a medical bill that will drain your finances.

農曆六月

(July 7th - August 6th) 己未
Your words may have the potential to offend if you are not careful enough this month, so make sure you are mindful of other peoples' sensibilities.

農曆七月

(August 7th - September 7th) 庚申
This is a good month for your Wealth Luck though you will need to continue engaging in teamwork for results.

農曆八月

(September 8th - October 7th) 辛酉
It may seem like you are working harder than ever this month, but you should do your best and persevere despite the stress.

農曆九月

(October 8th - November 6th) 壬戌
A promotion may come your way this month. There is no harm in asserting yourself and asking for what you have rightfully earned through hard work.

農曆十月

(November 7th - December 6th) 癸亥
It will be best for you to avoid making any major decisions this month that relate to money as this is a more suitable time for keeping your head down and waiting things out.

農曆十一月

(December 7th 2018 - January 4th 2019) 甲子
This is a good month for you to further your networking ventures, as the key to success is through the relationships you have forged.

農曆十二月

(January 5th - February 3rd 2019) 乙丑
New friends may present you with business opportunities and you will do well to listen to them and incorporate them into your plans strategically.

甲寅 Jia Yin Day

Overview

Be prepared for this to be a bumpy year for your wealth and career. However, a slight decrease in activity or slowing down of progress does not mean it is hopeless for you. Consider the fact that this downtime may be freeing up some of your resources and time, which you can use to invest in your education, through which you can adopt a new skill set and deepen your knowledge.

Wealth

Be strategic when it comes to managing your finances this year as your Wealth Luck may not be positive. Make sure you have a strong foundation to fall back on. Do research investments thoroughly and be more organised with your budget, and you will find that you do not encounter sudden financial problems.

Relationships

Single people may find that this is a good year to look for love. Patience is the key, even for those who are in a long-term relationship as honest communication is paramount this year. Talk openly about your feelings and make sure you also listen to your partner properly.

Health

You can rest assured that you will be mostly healthy this year, though you may want to keep an eye on your stress levels. Make sure you always make time for relaxing in your daily life or you may risk physical and mental exhaustion. Turn to nature for some downtime and peace.

Career

You are in a volatile place when it comes to your career. Faced with chaos and uncertainty, try looking within to rejuvenate your spirit and refocus on your goals. You may even discover some talents and come into the right mind to decide on the next step to take.

農曆正月

(February 4th - March 4th) 甲寅
You will find yourself constantly stressed this month, but you should not let it shake your life up too much. Find purpose in your daily life and stay motivated.

農曆二月

(March 5th - April 4th) 乙卯
Do not be tempted by a possible new job offer out there this month as impulsive decisions will come back to bite you in the back.

農曆三月

(April 5th - May 4th) 丙辰
This is a good month to tie up some loose ends and as such you should be proactive in your approach and get work done as soon as possible.

農曆四月

(May 5th - June 5th) 丁巳
Amp up your commitment and focus for your goals this month, so that you work on tasks that need to be done instead of getting distracted.

農曆五月

(June 6th - July 6th) 戊午
Watch out for possible eye-related problems this month. Furthermore, refrain from loaning money to anyone or being too generous than you can afford.

農曆六月

(July 7th - August 6th) 己未
Do not let yourself be pushed around by bullies who are trying to use you to get their way.

農曆七月

(August 7th - September 7th) 庚申
You will have a rollercoaster of emotions this month, which may cause confusion and disengagement from logic and reality.

農曆八月

(September 8th - October 7th) 辛酉
Do not get involved with the question of becoming someone's guarantor this month, as this will not bode well for you.

農曆九月

(October 8th - November 6th) 壬戌
Try not to let yourself be tempted by the impulsive urge to spend money this month. Be disciplined when it comes to shopping and avoid unnecessary expenditures.

農曆十月

(November 7th - December 6th) 癸亥
Even the darkest days will be met with light. Do not let negativity get you down as change is always around the corner.

農曆十一月

(December 7th 2018 - January 4th 2019) 甲子
Make sure you resolve all the loopholes in your work and see it to its proper completion. Be determined in finishing whatever it is you start.

農曆十二月

(January 5th - February 3rd 2019) 乙丑
You will have to try forging a positive relationship with a new superior at your workplace.

乙卯 Yi Mao Day

Overview

You may find that this is a year more for slowing down and recalibrating your senses. You will not find much success just waiting for positive outcomes to come your way as your business and career outlook is rather average. There may be much frustration and anxiety you have to deal with, and as such you should exercise patience and remember to keep the fight going for the future. Focus on your future goals and take into mind the work you need to put into achieving your goals.

 ## Wealth

Your wealth prospects this year are average at best, and there is a worst case scenario that you may lose money if you are not careful enough. If you have to make investments, make sure that you focus on education or self-improvement to enhance yourself as a resource. Hold out for now as eventually your wealth luck will resurface. Avoid other long-term investments as they will not yield great results.

 ## Relationships

Those who have been married for a while should think about relighting the fire in their relationship. Make sure to put in enough care and attention for your partner, and also think of new, fun ways you can enjoy each other's' company. Those who are single are advised to enjoy freedom as they will be better off single and focusing on themselves.

 ## Health

Your health will be more stable throughout the year, although you should not take anything for granted. Keep up with your medical check-ups and make sure you eat properly, accompanying a good diet with regular exercise. Your heart is an area of particular concern especially if you are above your thirties.

 ## Career

Your career advancement will be dependent on your ability to improve yourself. Consider signing up for new classes to enhance your skills and give you an edge over the competition. Treasure the fact that pursuing knowledge is a lifelong endeavour and despite bumps along the road, you will always have something to learn that will add to your overall quality of life.

農曆正月

(February 4th - March 4th) 甲寅
There may be more work for you to deal with this month, though you should look at it as an opportunity to showcase your skills.

農曆二月

(March 5th - April 4th) 乙卯
The workload will continue to increase this month, which could cause significant stress to you. Do make sure you take some time off every now and then.

農曆三月

(April 5th - May 4th) 丙辰
Steer clear of excessive overthinking as it will only further cloud your mind and delay you from making the right decisions.

農曆四月

(May 5th - June 5th) 丁巳
You may have to deal with unruly gossip this month. Try to avoid these people and do not let their negativity get to you.

農曆五月

(June 6th - July 6th) 戊午
This is good time for you to receive assistance from other people, as it is likely that the help you receive will be of exceptional quality.

農曆六月

(July 7th - August 6th) 己未
Avoid procrastination this month. Instead, make sure you are proactive in getting your tasks finished as soon as possible.

農曆七月

(August 7th - September 7th) 庚申
Your emotional state will be rather volatile this month, along with a general sense of moodiness. Do not let this negatively affect others.

農曆八月

(September 8th - October 7th) 辛酉
Do not isolate yourself from others and the potential assistance they may be able to offer you. There are trusted individuals in your life who can provide good advice and feedback.

農曆九月

(October 8th - November 6th) 壬戌
You will experience positive wealth luck this month, especially if you collaborate with others in group projects or partnerships.

農曆十月

(November 7th - December 6th) 癸亥
Stay away from pursuits in the stock market this month, as such risky investments will not do you any good.

農曆十一月

(December 7th 2018 - January 4th 2019) 甲子
There is a chance that you may experience some form of career advancement this month.

農曆十二月

(January 5th - February 3rd 2019) 乙丑
There is a possibility of a high usage of funds this month due to medical expenses, especially for those born in the summer.

丙辰 **Bing Chen Day**

Overview
The year of the Rooster year will prove to be a year of hectic progress for you. Naturally, exhaustion and stress come with the package, but you will also find some of this negativity coming from your family. Hence, you must occasionally take some time off to relax and recuperate. Once you get past the rough patches, it will be smooth sailing for you.

 ### Wealth
Be very careful with your investments this year as your wealth luck is unfavourable. Plan ahead and exercise prudence in your financial decisions, opting for budgeting over spending. That being said, those born during the summer are likely to be less affected.

 ### Relationships
This may be an ideal year to settle down and start families. However, in doing so, you must be level headed and compromising. Do not be too set in your ways that you do not take into consideration the concerns or ideas of others. Married women have potential problems they need to watch out for.

 ### Health
You should rethink your diet and get rid of unhealthy elements, especially if you were born during the winter. Junk food should definitely be removed from the menu. You may also want to consider going on a detoxification programme to cleanse your system so that you may start afresh. This will help you quell bad habits for the long term.

 ### Career
Your strict focus on your career goals this year will bear fruits for you. By shunning distractions, you will gain productivity and progress quickly. There is even a possible job promotion in the books for you if you remain committed to your goals.

農曆正月

(February 4th - March 4th) 甲寅
Your financial outlook is positive this month, as there may be a chance for you to cultivate a second or third source of income.

農曆二月

(March 5th - April 4th) 乙卯
Your financial luck will continue this month, and you should take full advantage of this by making the most of the opportunities that come your way.

農曆三月

(April 5th - May 4th) 丙辰
You may have trouble with communication this month. Your relations with others are unstable, especially when it comes to your superiors at work. Thus, you must do your best to foster understanding and cooperation instead.

農曆四月

(May 5th - June 5th) 丁巳
There may be some legal issues that crop up this month. Deal with them immediately instead of letting them fester and grow into something worse with more unfavourable outcomes.

農曆五月

(June 6th - July 6th) 戊午
Do not be afraid of seeking out the advice and opinions of others. There are supportive shoulders to lay on and willing ears that will gladly listen to your ideas and assist you with them.

農曆六月

(July 7th - August 6th) 己未
Look out for unhygienic food this month as there is a possibility of food poisoning. Be more careful with what you eat.

農曆七月

(August 7th - September 7th) 庚申
There is a chance that your spouse may do something that upsets you this month. However, you should not let emotions get the better of you and further escalate your problems.

農曆八月

(September 8th - October 7th) 辛酉
Be careful with legal documents this month especially those requiring a signature. Always read the fine print carefully before committing yourself to anything, as trouble may be spelled out in the tiny details.

農曆九月

(October 8th - November 6th) 壬戌
This is a month of clarity and balance, where you will find your emotions neutralizing into a calm plane. Self-awareness will come to you during this time and as such you should take advantage of this period and reflect carefully.

農曆十月

(November 7th - December 6th) 癸亥
Refrain from spontaneity and giving into impulse this month. It is better to be careful and think carefully before acting, This is not a good month for spontaneity.

農曆十一月

(December 7th 2018 - January 4th 2019) 甲子
No amount of money is worth breaking the rules for. You may be tempted to do so in order to take an easier or faster path to wealth, but refrain from doing so as the consequences will be heavy.

農曆十二月

(January 5th - February 3rd 2019) 乙丑
This will be a difficult month for married men as they will be tied down at work with a stringent schedule that takes them away from their family. Their families' needs will only add to the pressure one feels.

丁巳 **Ding Si Day**

Ding

Si

Overview

This is the perfect year for you to make some changes to your life and step out of your comfort zone. Do not be afraid to experiment with some new ideas and methods. Nevertheless, always exercise caution and attention to detail in your work even as you are innovating how you do your work. Creativity is the way to go as you seek out new experiences to improve your life and help you grow. Travelling will play a key role in helping you achieve this.

 ## Wealth

There will be an improvement to your work life this year that will improve your situation. Do not meet this prosperous change by doing the same things in the same ways, or by procrastinating and being complacent. Make sure you deal with any problems swiftly and continue to put in hard work and perseverance to ensure that you find wealth this year.

 ## Relationships

Single women will experience good Peach Blossom Luck this year. Married people should look out for the possibility of staleness in the relationship, which could cause tension and wandering eyes. Make sure you reignite the flames of your relationship by taking risks and doing something more exciting with each other.

 ## Health

Physically, a main feature of your health problems this year will be migraines and headaches caused by stress. Make sure you get yourself checked out and also watch out for potential head injuries. Aside from these concerns, your health outlook for the year is good.

 ## Career

There is a positive development in your career coming your way this year. Stay focused on your tasks and you will find that it is easier to accomplish your goals with strict discipline. Travelling will be advantageous, so make sure you seize the opportunities as they come your way.

農曆正月

(February 4th - March 4th) 甲寅
Use this month to try and make good impressions on others and showcase your talents. You will need to be confident enough to pull this off.

農曆二月

(March 5th - April 4th) 乙卯
Your Wealth Luck this month shines. Additionally, single men will find themselves blessed with many new romantic opportunities.

農曆三月

(April 5th - May 4th) 丙辰
You will be likely on the receiving end of some form of stressful career advancement this month, causing tension in your relationship.

農曆四月

(May 5th - June 5th) 丁巳
You should go and get yourself checked up for any possible ailments, as your heart is particularly prone to health issues.

農曆五月

(June 6th - July 6th) 戊午
Creative ideas will come easily to you this month, but you will need to be open enough to share them or else they will go to waste.

農曆六月

(July 7th - August 6th) 己未
Your personal relationships will be compromised this month by feelings of suspicion and insecurity. Communicate about your doubts honestly instead of speculating on your own.

農曆七月

(August 7th - September 7th) 庚申
You will be plagued by volatile emotions this month, which can only be mitigated by travel, particularly southwards.

農曆八月

(September 8th - October 7th) 辛酉
You have a rather strong wealth outlook this month, especially if you are born in the spring or summer. Teamwork is the way to go if you want to make the most of this time.

農曆九月

(October 8th - November 6th) 壬戌
You may begin to feel taken for granted by your superiors this month, much like your hard work is being ignored. Manage your emotions so that things do not get blown out of proportion.

農曆十月

(November 7th - December 6th) 癸亥
You will continue to be bothered by turbulent emotions this month, but you should try to stay focused and professional.

農曆十一月

(December 7th 2018 - January 4th 2019) 甲子
You will find yourself blessed with encouragement and support in your workplace, as well as good Wealth Luck.

農曆十二月

(January 5th - February 3rd 2019) 乙丑
Watch what you eat this month as there is a possibility of food poisoning.

戊午 **Wu Wu Day**

Overview

This year will be a relatively good year for you, especially when it comes to your wealth luck. You will have better luck being an employee rather than running your own business or working alone. It will do you good to take up new hobbies or try to learn something new, as a recharged skill set will benefit you in the future.

 ## Wealth

You are likely to be rewarded for your efforts at work through a pay raise. However, this money will not all come at once, but rather in steady increments that come as a result of careful decisions. Therefore, you should not spend too much in anticipating of a windfall. Steer clear of risky investments as well.

 ## Relationships

Men will have to deal with motherly interference in their relationships this year. Try to work at being a mediator between your partner and your mother so that conflicts are kept to a minimum. Those currently in long-term relationships will find that this is a good year to settle down.

 ## Health

You will lucky enough to experience good health this year. Do not take this for granted and instead work hard and maintaining your health. There is a risk of minor ailments involving your stomach and digestive system if you are not careful, especially with your eating habits.

 ## Career

This will be a prosperous year for your career and you see a lot of growth. The effort you have put into your work will finally pay off. You will also benefit from learning new skills or doing anything that that can help boost your professional standing.

農曆正月

(February 4th - March 4th) 甲寅
Do not be afraid to stand your ground and speak up for what is right and what you want. You certainly deserve some recognition and reward, especially in your career.

農曆二月

(March 5th - April 4th) 乙卯
Pregnant women have to be extra careful with their physical well-being this month as there is a risk of potential complications.

農曆三月

(April 5th - May 4th) 丙辰
Avoid procrastination or any form of idleness. Make sure you take care of all your important work as soon as possible. Stay active and plan ahead.

農曆四月

(May 5th - June 5th) 丁巳
Stay away from other peoples' drama this month, and do not let their words affect you. There is a chance you may dragged into someone else's gossip and get tangled up in their rumour mill.

農曆五月

(June 6th - July 6th) 戊午
You will be able to seek support and assistance from the opposite sex this month. Be gracious for their help and do not be surprised when they do offer their hand.

農曆六月

(July 7th - August 6th) 己未
Your stomach may become the source of some health problems this month. This can lead to mood swings if you are not more careful about your diet.

農曆七月

(August 7th - September 7th) 庚申
This is a month of chaos. Making the right decision is more difficult than ever. As such, take a step back and evaluate yourself rather than feeling compelled to make hasty decisions.

農曆八月

(September 8th - October 7th) 辛酉
You will have to maintain your restraint in not making impulsive decisions again this month. Your ego and pride in particular are problematic areas you need to watch out for.

農曆九月

(October 8th - November 6th) 壬戌
Engage in beneficial teamwork this month in order to see some progress at your workplace and with your finances, with less burden on your shoulders.

農曆十月

(November 7th - December 6th) 癸亥
If you are a businessperson or an entrepreneur, look to go abroad for business deals or agreements as they are more lucrative than ever this month.

農曆十一月

(December 7th 2018 - January 4th 2019) 甲子
You may find yourself facing a slew of social obligations this month, which may be accompanied by the temptation to overindulge on food and alcohol.

農曆十二月

(January 5th - February 3rd 2019) 乙丑
Single women will have better luck this month in meeting prospective partners. Do not hesitate to make the first move and charm them by being yourself.

己未 Ji Wei Day

Overview

You will experience a better health outlook this year. In addition, Noble People will also be more than willing to assist you in your endeavours. With this assistance available to you, you should restrain yourself from following your impulses as there are plenty of opportunities to go through proper consultations first, especially with financial investments. Aside from this, you will also have the chance to break old habits and cultivate better ones that will prove useful to you in the long run.

 ## Wealth

Pursue creative avenues for wealth this year and you will be rewarded for your innovation and fearlessness. If you are in a partnership, you will need to be careful with your communications and refrain from offending the other parties. There is a possibility that you will have to settle for less, but appreciate the opportunity to sustain your business or project regardless. Be thankful rather than resentful as in the end, all this will pay off.

 ## Relationships

Single men may be able to enjoy good romantic luck this year, while women in a relationship may find themselves facing off with their significant other regarding some conflict. Additionally, they will also encounter a potentially difficult situation involving their partner and an old friend. Deal with this sensitive situation using patience and compassion rather than anger and suspicion.

 ## Health

Those born in the spring may experience exceptional health. Everyone else needs to watch out for stomach-related issues such as food poisoning. These stomach problems could turn out to be recurring.

 ## Career

Keep a low profile at work this year to avoid as many scandals and arguments as possible. Though there appear to many opportunities for you to speak up and shine, it would be wiser for you to hold back and be patient. Eventually, your humility and patience may pay off in the form of some career advancement in June.

農曆正月

(February 4th - March 4th) 甲寅
Now is the time for you to venture into new horizons and try something new. This may come in the form of a new partnership.

農曆二月

(March 5th - April 4th) 乙卯
Be careful with your words this month as there is the chance that you will cause serious offence to someone else. Restrain yourself from making immediate judgements or conclusions.

農曆三月

(April 5th - May 4th) 丙辰
Your workplace stress will come to a head this month as competition heats up. There is still a chance for you to not be left behind if you stay determined to get ahead of the learning curve.

農曆四月

(May 5th - June 5th) 丁巳
You will need to be more careful when you are travelling this month as there is a chance that you may encounter an accident. Do not let yourself be easily distracted and keep your safety as a priority.

農曆五月

(June 6th - July 6th) 戊午
There may be a promotion waiting for you this month. Recognise that your hard work has finally paid off and take this as a lesson that all labour will eventually bear fruits.

農曆六月

(July 7th - August 6th) 己未
Stay out of legal complications this month by being cautious and wary of suspicious situations. Avoid getting tangled in other people's problems and do not let yourself be pressured into getting involved either as it will not be worth it.

農曆七月

(August 7th - September 7th) 庚申
This is not a good month for financial investments as the situation is rather unreadable right now. There is a chance that the market is in a unstable state and investments at this point will be entirely unbeneficial.

農曆八月

(September 8th - October 7th) 辛酉
Pregnant women are at risk of potential health issues this month and as such they will need to be more cautious and careful.

農曆九月

(October 8th - November 6th) 壬戌
You may find yourself quarrelling with your significant other a lot this month on your finances. Try to mitigate these disagreement early on as such arguments will lead to a point of no return. If the situation still escalates, do not lose your temper.

農曆十月

(November 7th - December 6th) 癸亥
Malicious gossip and rumours about you are abound. Those you once trusted may end up backstabbing you or spreading more lies. Be selective in who you let into your inner circle and do your best to ignore these vicious individuals.

農曆十一月

(December 7th 2018 - January 4th 2019) 甲子
It will not be good for you to be seen as a nonchalant or uncaring person. Make sure that you behave in a way that in mindful and considerate so that people do not perceive you as insensitive and unreliable.

農曆十二月

(January 5th - February 3rd 2019) 乙丑
Avoid procrastination as much as you can as such behaviour will only come back to bite you. Finish your work as soon as the opportunity is available so that you pace yourself properly.

庚申 Geng Shen Day

庚 Geng
申 Shen

Overview

Your year ahead is looking more positive as your efforts over the years begin to pay off, particularly if you are professional or consider yourself a white-collar worker. Keep up your efforts in order to continue building your foundation and solidifying your reputation.

 Wealth

You need to understand how important pro-activeness is when it comes to financial matters. Let loose your adventurous side and pursue endeavours that you might never have thought about before. Try out new approaches and get creative with your methods to yield interesting results.

 Relationships

If you are in a long-term relationship or are married, you may experience quite a bit of emotional turmoil. You will need to be very patient in dealing with this so that you do not lose your temper and cause a bigger rift. Choose your battles wisely and opt for compromise.

 Health

You may likely be plagued by blood-related illnesses and skin allergies. As such, you will need to get regular medical check-ups and maintain a healthy diet, being wary of stomach and food poisoning issues as well. If ignored, these issues could develop into chronic problems. Rethink your dietary habits and make changes accordingly.

 Career

You may start to think about changing jobs or positions. Travel is also a possibility, especially if it is work related. Be more flexible and open-minded during these endeavours. If you own a business, you must be more alert than usual as there may be problems within your organisation that you will have to curb early on.

農曆正月

(February 4th - March 4th) 甲寅
Those who own their own businesses will find that this is a difficult and competitive month. There is a chance they may lose some of their valuable staff.

農曆二月

(March 5th - April 4th) 乙卯
Strong competition continues on this month, especially for those born in the summer. Re-evaluate your plans and think of new ways to combat your competitors.

農曆三月

(April 5th - May 4th) 丙辰
Steer clear of hasty decisions this month and instead adopt the habit of thinking carefully to avoid future regrets.

農曆四月

(May 5th - June 5th) 丁巳
Try to ignore potential stress this month or you risk getting too affected and succumbing to stress-related skin problems, such as rashes or other allergies. Learn how to let go every once in a while.

農曆五月

(June 6th - July 6th) 戊午
You will experience positive Wealth Luck this month especially if you were born in the winter. Use this to your advantage – for instance, if you feel a pay raise is long overdue, now is the time to ask for one.

農曆六月

(July 7th - August 6th) 己未
Your auspicious Wealth Luck continues on this month and as such, you should take this opportunity to think of new ideas to implement.

農曆七月

(August 7th - September 7th) 庚申
Steer clear of rule breaking or unethical shortcuts this month as it will only lead to future legal troubles.

農曆八月

(September 8th - October 7th) 辛酉
Those who were born in the autumn or winter will benefit greatly from working in close collaboration with others this month.

農曆九月

(October 8th - November 6th) 壬戌
Arguments may crop up this month between you and your significant other, with jealousy and insecurity being the most serious motivating factors.

農曆十月

(November 7th - December 6th) 癸亥
Your emotions are chaotic this month, making it difficult for you to stay focused. Seek unbiased perspectives from others so that you can recalibrate your thoughts and make better decisions.

農曆十一月

(December 7th 2018 - January 4th 2019) 甲子
This is a good month for becoming involved in partnerships and joint ventures. Take up the opportunity should it present itself.

農曆十二月

(January 5th - February 3rd 2019) 乙丑
You will find yourself rather stressed this month, though you should not let it get to you. You can step back every once in a while to recover your mind.

辛酉 Xin You Day

Overview

This will likely be a rough year for you especially when it comes to your career. Your workplace is likely infested with petty individuals who will try to bring you down due to their own jealousy and incapability. You will need to keep a low profile while continuing to work hard to nullify their efforts. Stay calm even in the face of being demanded to explain yourself.

 ## Wealth

Your Wealth Luck is in a good place, though this means people will want to get close to you for dubious reasons. Protect yourself against their pretension by just doing your own thing. Matters will improve by the second half of the year particularly for those born in the spring or summer.

 ## Relationships

Your relationships will only work out if you put enough effort into them. Men in particular must remember to neglect their partner in the pursuit of other interests, or your spouse may look elsewhere for attention. Women will have to exercise more patience this year to make their relationships work. Nevertheless, the second half of the year will bring better Peach Blossom Luck.

 ## Health

You will need to be more careful with your health and be on the lookout for your blood pressure, heart and eyes. Women may experience gynaecological health problems this year as well. As such, you should go for a full medical check-up to anticipate possible complications.

 ## Career

Do keep your head down and focus on your work this year. Keep a low profile as there are unscrupulous people out there who are looking for people to use. They may try to claim your ideas as their own. Try to be more discerning of you who trust. Additionally, make sure you ensure that your work is exemplary and thorough so that you are not faulted unnecessarily.

農曆正月

(February 4th - March 4th) 甲寅
The month will start off bumpily at work for you due to some colleagues trying to rob you of your ideas and take all the credit.

農曆二月

(March 5th - April 4th) 乙卯
Pregnant women may face some complications this month. Do not take any risks and make sure you are more careful and see your doctor at the first sign of trouble.

農曆三月

(April 5th - May 4th) 丙辰
You need to follow up new ideas with planning and execution. This way, you can yield solid results and gain valuable experience from trying new things.

農曆四月

(May 5th - June 5th) 丁巳
While you may experience auspicious Wealth Luck this month, you will need to exercise more caution if you are travelling.

農曆五月

(June 6th - July 6th) 戊午
Your Wealth Luck will continue to prosper this month. Unfortunately, this might cause others to envy and resent your good fortune. Make sure you cut off these toxic people and focus on yourself.

農曆六月

(July 7th - August 6th) 己未
This will be a taxing month for men in relationships, as you encounter many arguments with your spouse. Angry outbursts may bring momentary satisfaction but it will not do any good.

農曆七月

(August 7th - September 7th) 庚申
Your luck with your career is looking good this month, which means that you may receive a promotion or other benefits this month.

農曆八月

(September 8th - October 7th) 辛酉
Avoid making major decisions this month, especially if they involve the law.

農曆九月

(October 8th - November 6th) 壬戌
You should try enrolling in a course to pick up a new language or learn something new in order to stimulate your brain and bring momentum and inspiration to your life.

農曆十月

(November 7th - December 6th) 癸亥
Social activity will clog your schedule this month, and as such you will need to moderate your partying and indulgence.

農曆十一月

(December 7th 2018 - January 4th 2019) 甲子
You may find yourself locking heads with your superiors this month, but you should refrain from complaining behind their backs and risk being seen as undiplomatic and unprofessional.

農曆十二月

(January 5th - February 3rd 2019) 乙丑
Heart problems are the focus of your health issues this month. If you are over forty years of age, you should go for a medical screening to catch the problem early.

壬戌 **Ren Xu Day**

Ren

Xu

Overview

A partnership or joint-venture will enable a career or business advancement for you this year. It will be beneficial for you to set up a strong network of trusted and experienced individuals who can help you along in your endeavours. This way your burden is lessened and you can share ideas and responsibilities with others, making your resources better managed. Be more open and attentive towards what others can bring to the table.

 ### Wealth

You will find it hard to make money this year. You need to stay ahead of the game by creating opportunities for yourself and revising old approaches to increase efficiency in the workplace. The power of multiple minds will get a lot done, too, so try to collaborate with others and work towards financial improvement.

 ### Relationships

You may find yourself meeting a significant through one of your friends. However, for those who are already in relationships, trouble looms. There is a possibility of betrayal and third-party interference. As such, you should try to keep the lines of communication open and stay alert for possible issues in your relationship so you can nip them in the bud.

 ### Health

Youngsters will not find themselves troubled by health problems this year. However, older folks will have to pay attention to their blood sugar levels. An important step to take is to adjust your diet so that you are healthier and less at risk of sudden health issues due to overindulgence in sugar or cholesterol.

 ### Career

Competition is abound at the workplace and as such you will find yourself more easily stressed. Do surround yourself with the people you trust and who you are comfortable with so that they can help you bear this burden and fend off attention from the wrong people. Being alone will only worsen your situation and as such you should do your best to strengthen your relationships.

農曆正月

(February 4th - March 4th) 甲寅
Feeling of jealousy plague you at the workplace this month as others begin spreading rumours that your superiors unfairly favour another colleague over everyone else. Do not let perceptions cloud your judgment and keep you from focusing on the task at hand as you should not let yourself be bogged down by these negative feelings.

農曆二月

(March 5th - April 4th) 乙卯
Do not be afraid to share your ideas this month. Have faith in their legitimacy and be confident that they will be positively received and that you will get good feedback that will help you work on future ideas

農曆三月

(April 5th - May 4th) 丙辰
There is a potential for workplace discord this month as you butt heads with your colleagues over disagreements. Try to resolve these arguments as cordially as possible so that the situation does not worsen beyond your control.

農曆四月

(May 5th - June 5th) 丁巳
You may be financially rewarded this month for all the hard work that you have invested into a side project. This is a lesson that diligence and good decisions will always pay off.

農曆五月

(June 6th - July 6th) 戊午
You will be faced with a busy month and as such you need to know when to take a break and unwind as mental stress can always lead to poor physical health. You may fall ill this month, but you can mitigate some of the negative effects by taking time off.

農曆六月

(July 7th - August 6th) 己未
Watch your words and be mindful of other peoples' sensibilities as there is a risk of you offending someone with harsh or careless words.

農曆七月

(August 7th - September 7th) 庚申
Financial rewards will grace you this month alongside with an increase of financial luck. This is especially true for individuals born during the summer.

農曆八月

(September 8th - October 7th) 辛酉
New opportunities will come to you through business travel. As such, do not be afraid to take that step and also keep your eyes peeled for such opportunities.

農曆九月

(October 8th - November 6th) 壬戌
You will find yourself fatigued by a sense of discontent and jadedness. Do not wait for this restless feeling to dissipate on its own, instead reflect on what brought you this place and avoid acting out as that will not solve the problem, but only worsen it.

農曆十月

(November 7th - December 6th) 癸亥
Do not let yourself get distracted from the things that matter. There will be no shortage of chaos around you, and as such you should try to distance yourself from such possible distractions for a while so you can clear your head.

農曆十一月

(December 7th 2018 - January 4th 2019) 甲子
Travel in the south this month to reap rewards for your professional life and gain more opportunities that can bring great rewards.

農曆十二月

(January 5th - February 3rd 2019) 乙丑
Be on the alert for possible tips and tricks circling around from your colleagues as this is likely to result in some good ideas that can come in handy for the future when you are looking for new projects to take on.

癸亥 Gui Hai Day

Overview

This year will prove auspicious for you as your hard work begins to pay off and you find yourself rewarded handsomely. This does not mean it is time for you to retire your efforts as there is still much to do. Keep your momentum going and lay a strong foundation for the future. It would be wise for you to look out for collaborations and opportunities for teamwork this year as this will help you move up in the world more efficiently.

 ### Wealth

It would be best for you to gun for assignments that involve teamwork and co-operation as it will help boost your productivity. Try to think about your work in terms of why you love doing it, not in terms of the financial rewards as this can lead to greed and cause you to neglect your passions.

Relationships

Single individuals will find their romantic luck in full bloom this year. There is a chance of meeting your future partner at work or through some professional networks or event. Do not give up even if you are met with a few disappointments. If you persevere, true love may come your way this year.

 ### Health

Your heavy workload may negatively impact your health. It will be wise for you to remember that your health is just as important to your happiness as your career is. Do not be afraid to take a break every now and then so that you have time for yourself to recuperate and recharge your momentum.

 ### Career

Be prudent with the resources available to you this year so that your work is always effective and efficient. Work at forming networks with important individuals and do not be afraid to share your successes and rewards with the people who have helped you reach where you want to be. If you undertake all your endeavours alone, it will not be as rewarding or fulfilling.

農曆正月

(February 4th - March 4th) 甲寅
There will be much for you to accomplish this month but you should view this in perspective to the rest of your life so you do not overwork yourself.

農曆二月

(March 5th - April 4th) 乙卯
This is a good time for you to take some of your ideas and present them to your peers for their feedback and possible collaboration.

農曆三月

(April 5th - May 4th) 丙辰
Do not give in to laziness this month. There is a temptation to let things slide, but if you do not stand your ground you will end up regretting it as you will not be able to get any work done.

農曆四月

(May 5th - June 5th) 丁巳
Your legs are at risk of encountering injury this month. As such, you will need to be careful whenever engaging in sports or other activities. Pregnant women will also need to watch out for potential accidents.

農曆五月

(June 6th - July 6th) 戊午
This is a good month for new beginnings. As such, go ahead and try something new and innovate on old ideas. With your creativity flowing freely, you will find that your momentum gets charged up again.

農曆六月

(July 7th - August 6th) 己未
Chaos is abound this month, piling stress onto your fatigued shoulders. You will need to remember the potential negative implications of stress on your health and do your best to mitigate those impacts.

農曆七月

(August 7th - September 7th) 庚申
You may face some financial difficulty this month which you will need to deal with immediately to prevent the effects from spreading too far.

農曆八月

(September 8th - October 7th) 辛酉
There will be a series of problems that catch you off guard and pull you into a cycle of stress this month. You will be prone to irritation, but you need to keep your temper in check and remember to stay calm.

農曆九月

(October 8th - November 6th) 壬戌
This month will see you bring a long-suffering project at work to fruition and finally be able to reap the reward of having worked so hard.

農曆十月

(November 7th - December 6th) 癸亥
You will be confronted by more work this month which you will need to learn to balance with the rest of your life. Stay calm in the face of adversity and you will pull through.

農曆十一月

(December 7th 2018 - January 4th 2019) 甲子
You will receive confusing remarks from a friend this month that will cause hurt. Try to be less sensitive so that you approach the situation with a more open mind as it is not worth losing a friendship over.

農曆十二月

(January 5th - February 3rd 2019) 乙丑
There is a possibility that rumours are circling about you, likely spread by individuals who want to damage your reputation. You simply have to keep moving forward and put them in the past.

JOEY YAP CONSULTING GROUP

Pioneering Metaphysics-Centric Personal and Corporate Consultations

Founded in 2002, the Joey Yap Consulting Group is the pioneer in the provision of metaphysics-driven coaching and consultation services for professionals and individuals alike. Under the leadership of the renowned international Chinese Metaphysics consultant, author and trainer, Dato' Joey Yap, it has become a world-class specialised metaphysics consulting firm with a strong presence in four continents, meeting the metaphysics-centric needs of its A-list clientele, ranging from celebrities to multinational corporations.

The Group's core consultation practice areas include Feng Shui, BaZi and Qi Men Dun Jia, which are complemented by ancillary services such as Date Selection, Face Reading and Yi Jing. Its team of highly trained professional consultants, led by its Chief Consultant, Dato' Joey Yap, is well-equipped with unparalleled knowledge and experience to help clients achieve their ultimate potentials in various fields and specialisations. Given its credentials, the Group is certainly the firm of choice across the globe for metaphysics-related consultations.

The Peerless Industry Expert

Benchmarked against the standards of top international consulting firms, our consultants work closely with our clients to achieve the best possible outcomes. The possibilities are infinite as our expertise extends from consultations related to the forces of nature under the subject of Feng Shui, to those related to Destiny Analysis and effective strategising under BaZi and Qi Men Dun Jia respectively.

To date, we have consulted a great diversity of clients, ranging from corporate clients – from various industries such as real estate, finance and telecommunication, amongst others – to the hundreds of thousands of individuals in their key life aspects. Adopting up-to-date and pragmatic approaches, we provide comprehensive services while upholding the importance of clients' priorities and effective outcomes. Recognised as the epitome of Chinese Metaphysics, we possess significant testimonies from worldwide clients as a trusted Brand.

Feng Shui Consultation

Residential Properties
- Initial Land/Property Assessment
- Residential Feng Shui Consultation
- Residential Land Selection
- End-to-End Residential Consultation

Commercial Properties
- Initial Land/Property Assessment
- Commercial Feng Shui Consultation
- Commercial Land Selection
- End-to-End Commercial Consultation

Property Developers
- End-to-End Consultation
- Post-Consultation Advisory Services
- Panel Feng Shui Consultant

Property Investors
- Your Personal Feng Shui Consultant
- Tailor-Made Packages

Memorial Parks & Burial Sites
- Yin House Feng Shui

BaZi Consultation

Personal Destiny Analysis
- Individual BaZi Analysis
- BaZi Analysis for Families

Strategic Analysis for Corporate Organizations
- BaZi Consultations for Corporations
- BaZi Analysis for Human Resource Management

Entrepreneurs and Business Owners
- BaZi Analysis for Entrepreneurs

Career Pursuits
- BaZi Career Analysis

Relationships
- Marriage and Compatibility Analysis
- Partnership Analysis

General Public
- Annual BaZi Forecast
- Your Personal BaZi Coach

Date Selection Consultation

- **Marriage Date Selection**
- **Caesarean Birth Date Selection**
- **House-Moving Date Selection**
- **Renovation and Groundbreaking Dates**
- **Signing of Contracts**
- **O icial Openings**
- **Product Launches**

Qi Men Dun Jia Consultation

Strategic Execution
- Business and Investment Prospects

Forecasting
- Wealth and Life Pursuits
- People and Environmental Matters

Feng Shui
- Residential Properties
- Commercial Properties

Speaking Engagement

Many reputable organisations and institutions have worked closely with Joey Yap Consulting Group to build a synergistic business relationship by engaging our team of consultants, which are led by Joey Yap, as speakers at their corporate events.

We tailor our seminars and talks to suit the anticipated or pertinent group of audience. Be it department subsidiary, your clients or even the entire corporation, we aim to fit your requirements in delivering the intended message(s) across.

CHINESE METAPHYSICS REFERENCE SERIES

The Chinese Metaphysics Reference Series is a collection of reference texts, source material, and educational textbooks to be used as supplementary guides by scholars, students, researchers, teachers and practitioners of Chinese Metaphysics.

These comprehensive and structured books provide fast, easy reference to aid in the study and practice of various Chinese Metaphysics subjects including Feng Shui, BaZi, Yi Jing, Zi Wei, Liu Ren, Ze Ri, Ta Yi, Qi Men Dun Jia and Mian Xiang.

The Chinese Metaphysics Compendium

At over 1,000 pages, the Chinese Metaphysics Compendium is a unique one-volume reference book that compiles ALL the formulas relating to Feng Shui, BaZi (Four Pillars of Destiny), Zi Wei (Purple Star Astrology), Yi Jing (I-Ching), Qi Men (Mystical Doorways), Ze Ri (Date Selection), Mian Xiang (Face Reading) and other sources of Chinese Metaphysics.

It is presented in the form of easy-to-read tables, diagrams and reference charts, all of which are compiled into one handy book. This first-of-its-kind compendium is presented in both English and its original Chinese language, so that none of the meanings and contexts of the technical terminologies are lost.

The only essential and comprehensive reference on Chinese Metaphysics, and an absolute must-have for all students, scholars, and practitioners of Chinese Metaphysics.

The Ten Thousand Year Calendar (Pocket Edition)

The Ten Thousand Year Calendar

Dong Gong Date Selection

The Date Selection Compendium

Plum Blossoms Divination Reference Book

Xuan Kong Da Gua Ten Thousand Year Calendar

San Yuan Dragon Gate Eight Formations Water Method

BaZi Hour Pillar Useful Gods - Wood

BaZi Hour Pillar Useful Gods - Fire

BaZi Hour Pillar Useful Gods - Earth

BaZi Hour Pillar Useful Gods - Metal

BaZi Hour Pillar Useful Gods - Water

Xuan Kong Da Gua Structures Reference Book

Xuan Kong Da Gua 64 Gua Transformation Analysis

BaZi Structures and Structural Useful Gods - Wood

BaZi Structures and Structural Useful Gods - Fire

BaZi Structures and Structural Useful Gods - Earth

BaZi Structures and Structural Useful Gods - Metal

BaZi Structures and Structural Useful Gods - Water

Earth Study Discern Truth Second Edition

Eight Mansions Bright Mirror

Secret of Xuan Kong

Ode to Flying Stars

Xuan Kong Purple White Script

Ode to Mysticism

The Yin House Handbook

Water Water Everywhere

Xuan Kong Da Gua Not Exactly For Dummies

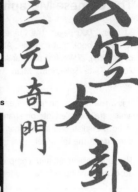

Joey Yap's BaZi Profiling System

Three Levels of BaZi Profiling (English & Chinese versions)

In BaZi Profiling, there are three levels that reflect three different stages of a person's personal nature and character structure.

Level 1 – The Day Master

The Day Master in a nutshell is the basic you. The inborn personality. It is your essential character. It answers the basic question "who am I". There are ten basic personality profiles – the ten Day Masters – each with its unique set of personality traits, likes and dislikes.

Level 2 – The Structure

The Structure is your behavior and attitude – in other words, it is about how you use your personality. It expands on the Day Master (Level 1). The structure reveals your natural tendencies in life – are you a controller, creator, supporter, thinker or connector? Each of the Ten Day Masters express themselves differently through the five Structures. Why do we do the things we do? Why do we like the things we like? The answers are in our BaZi Structure.

Level 3 – The Profile

The Profile depicts your role in your life. There are ten roles (Ten BaZi Profiles) related to us. As to each to his or her own - the roles we play are different from one another and it is unique to each Profile.

What success means to you, for instance, differs from your friends – this is similar to your sense of achievement or whatever you think of your purpose in life is.

Through the BaZi Profile, you will learn the deeper level of your personality. It helps you become aware of your personal strengths and works as a trigger for you to make all the positive changes to be a better version of you.

Keep in mind, only through awareness that you will be able to maximise your natural talents, abilities and skills. Only then, ultimately, you will get to enter into what we refer as 'flow' of life – a state where you have the powerful force to naturally succeed in life.

THE BaZi
60 PILLARS SERIES

The BaZi 60 Pillars Series is a collection of ten volumes focusing on each of the Pillars or Jia Zi in BaZi Astrology. Learn how to see BaZi Chart in a new light through the Pictorial Method of BaZi analysis and elevate your proficiency in BaZi studies through this new understanding. Joey Yap's 60 Pillars Life Analysis Method is a refined and enhanced technique that is based on the fundamentals set by the true masters of olden times, and modified to fit to the sophistication of current times.

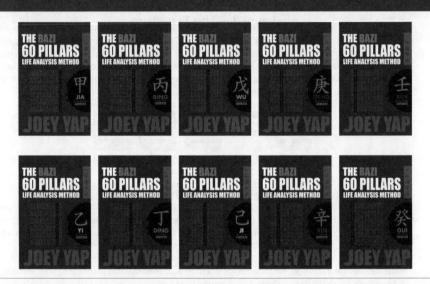

BaZi Collection

With these books, leading Chinese Astrology Master Trainer Joey Yap makes it easy to learn how to unlock your Destiny through your BaZi. BaZi or Four Pillars of Destiny is an ancient Chinese science which enables individuals to understand their personality, hidden talents and abilities, as well as their luck cycle - by examining the information contained within their birth data.

Understand and learn more about this accurate ancient science with this BaZi Collection.

BOOK 1   BOOK 2   BOOK 3   BOOK 4   BOOK 5   The 10 Gods

(Available in English & Chinese)

Feng Shui Collection

Design Your Legacy

Design Your Legacy is Joey Yap's first book on the profound subject of Yin House Feng Shui, which is the study Feng Shui for burials and tombs. Although it is still pretty much a hidden practice that is largely unexplored by modern literature, the significance of Yin House Feng Shui has permeated through the centuries – from the creation of the imperial lineage of emperors in ancient times to the iconic leaders who founded modern China.

This book unveils the true essence of Yin House Feng Shui with its significant applications that are unlike the myths and superstition which have for years, overshadowed the genuine practice itself. Discover how Yin House Feng Shui – the true precursor to all modern Feng Shui practice, can be used to safeguard the future of your descendants and create a lasting legacy.

Must-Haves for Property Analysis!

For homeowners, those looking to build their own home or even investors who are looking to apply Feng Shui to their homes, these series of books provides valuable information from the classical Feng Shui therioes and applications.

In his trademark straight-to-the-point manner, Joey shares with you the Feng Shui do's and dont's when it comes to finding a property with favorable Feng Shui, which is condusive for home living.

Stories and Lessons on Feng Shui Series

All in all, this series is a delightful chronicle of Joey's articles, thoughts and vast experience - as a professional Feng Shui consultant and instructor - that have been purposely refined, edited and expanded upon to make for a light-hearted, interesting yet educational read. And with Feng Shui, BaZi, Mian Xiang and Yi Jing all thrown into this one dish, there's something for everyone.

(Available in English & Chinese)

More Titles under Joey Yap Books

Pure Feng Shui

Pure Feng Shui is Joey Yap's debut with an international publisher, CICO Books. It is a refreshing and elegant look at the intricacies of Classical Feng Shui - now compiled in a useful manner for modern day readers. This book is a comprehensive introduction to all the important precepts and techniques of Feng Shui practices.

Your Aquarium Here

This book is the first in Fengshuilogy Series, which is a series of matter-of-fact and useful Feng Shui books designed for the person who wants to do a fuss-free Feng Shui.

Walking the Dragons

Compiled in one book for the first time from Joey Yap's Feng Shui Mastery Excursion Series, the book highlights China's extensive, vibrant history with astute observations on the Feng Shui of important sites and places. Learn the landform formations of Yin Houses (tombs and burial places), as well as mountains, temples, castles and villages.

Walking the Dragons : Taiwan Excursion

A Guide to Classical Landform Feng Shui of Taiwan

From China to Tibet, Joey Yap turns his analytical eye towards Taiwan in this extensive Walking the Dragons series. Combined with beautiful images and detailed information about an island once known as Formosa, or "Beautiful Island" in Portuguese, this compelling series of essays highlights the colourful history and wonders of Taiwan. It also provides readers with fascinating insights into the living science of Feng Shui.

The Art of Date Selection: Personal Date Selection (Available in English & Chinese)

With the Art of Date Selection: Personal Date Selection, you can learn simple, practical methods to select not just good dates, but personalised good dates as well. Whether it is a personal activity such as a marriage or professional endeavour, such as launching a business - signing a contract or even acquiring assets, this book will show you how to pick the good dates and tailor them to suit the activity in question, and to avoid the negative ones too!

Your Head Here

Your Head Here is the first book by Sherwin Ng. She is an accomplished student of Joey Yap, and an experienced Feng Shui consultant and instructor with Joey Yap Consulting Group and Mastery Academy respectively. It is the second book under the Fengshuilogy series, which focuses on Bedroom Feng Shui, a specific topic dedicated to optimum bed location and placement.

If the Shoe Fits

This book is for those who want to make the effort to enhance their relationship.

In her debut release, Jessie Lee humbly shares with you the classical BaZi method of the Ten Day Masters and the combination of a new profiling system developed by Joey Yap, to understand and deal with the people around you.

Being Happy and Successful at Work and in your Career

Have you ever wondered why some of us are so successful in our careers while others are dragging their feet to work or switching from one job to another? Janet Yung hopes to answer this question by helping others through the knowledge and application of BaZi and Chinese Astrology. In her debut release, she shares with the readers the right way of using BaZi to understand themselves: their inborn talents, motivations, skills, and passions, to find their own place in the path of professional development.

Being Happy & Successful - Managing Yourself & Others

Manage Your Talent & Have Effective Relationships at the Workplace

While many strive for efficiency in the workplace, it is vital to know how to utilize your talents. In this book, Janet Yung will take you further on how to use the BaZi profiling system as a tool to assess your personality and understanding your approach to the job. From ways in communicating with your colleagues to understanding your boss, you will be astounded by what this ancient system can reveal about you and the people in your life. Tips and guidance will also be given in this book so that you will make better decisions for your next step in advancing in your career.

Face Reading Collection

The Chinese Art of Face Reading: The Book of Moles

The Book of Moles by Joey Yap delves into the inner meanings of moles and what they reveal about the personality and destiny of an individual. Complemented by fascinating illustrations and Joey Yap's easy-to-understand commentaries and guides, this book takes a deeper focus into a Face Reading subject, which can be used for everyday decisions – from personal relationships to professional dealings and many others.

Discover Face Reading (Available in English & Chinese)

This is a comprehensive book on all areas of Face Reading, covering some of the most important facial features, including the forehead, mouth, ears and even philtrum above your lips. This book will help you analyse not just your Destiny but also help you achieve your full potential and achieve life fulfillment.

Joey Yap's Art of Face Reading

The Art of Face Reading is Joey Yap's second effort with CICO Books, and it takes a lighter, more practical approach to Face Reading. This book does not focus on the individual features as it does on reading the entire face. It is about identifying common personality types and characters.

Faces of Fortune: The 20 Tycoons to bet on over the next 10 years

Faces of Fortune is Tee Lin Say's first book on the subject of Mian Xiang or Chinese Face Reading. As an accomplished Face Reading student of Joey Yap and an experienced business journalist, Lin Say merged both her knowledge into this volume, profiling twenty prominent tycoons in Asia based on the Art of Face Reading.

Easy Guide on Face Reading (Available in English & Chinese)

The Face Reading Essentials series of books comprises of five individual books on the key features of the face – the Eyes, the Eyebrows, the Ears, the Nose, and the Mouth. Each book provides a detailed illustration and a simple yet descriptive explanation on the individual types of the features.

The books are equally useful and effective for beginners, enthusiasts and those who are curious. The series is designed to enable people who are new to Face Reading to make the most out of first impressions and learn to apply Face Reading skills to understand the personality and character of their friends, family, co-workers and business associates.

2018 Annual Releases

Chinese Astrology for 2018   Feng Shui for 2018   Tong Shu Desktop Calendar 2018   Qi Men Desktop Calendar 2018   Professional Tong Shu Diary 2018   Tong Shu Monthly Planner 2018   Weekly Tong Shu Diary 2018

Discover the True Significance of the Ancient Art of Lion Dance

The Lion has long been a symbol of power and strength. That powerful symbol has evolved into an incredible display of a mixture of martial arts and ritualism that is the Lion Dance. Throughout ancient and modern times, the Lion Dance has stamped itself as a popular part of culture, but is there a meaning lost behind this magnificent spectacle?

The Art of Lion Dance written by the world's number one man in Chinese Metaphysics, Dato' Joey Yap, explains the history and origins of the art and its connection to Qi Men Dun Jia. By creating that bridge with Qi Men, the Lion Dance is able to ritualise any type of ceremony, celebrations and mourning alike.

The book is the perfect companion to the modern interpretation of the art as it reveals the significance behind each part of the Lion costume, as well as rituals that are put in place to bring the costume and its spectacle to life.

Educational Tools and Software

Joey Yap's Feng Shui Template Set

Directions are the cornerstone of any successful Feng Shui audit or application. The Joey Yap Feng Shui Template Set is a set of three templates to simplify the process of taking directions and determining locations and positions, whether it is for a building, a house, or an open area such as a plot of land - all of it done with just a floor plan or area map.

The Set comprises three basic templates: The Basic Feng Shui Template, Eight Mansions Feng Shui Template, and the Flying Stars Feng Shui Template.

Mini Feng Shui Compass

The Mini Feng Shui Compass is a self-aligning compass that is not only light at 100gms but also built sturdily to ensure it will be convenient to use anywhere. The rings on the Mini Feng Shui Compass are bilingual and incorporate the 24 Mountain Rings that is used in your traditional Luo Pan.

The comprehensive booklet included with this, will guide you in applying the 24 Mountain Directions on your Mini Feng Shui Compass effectively and the Eight Mansions Feng Shui to locate the most auspicious locations within your home, office and surroundings. You can also use the Mini Feng Shui Compass when measuring the direction of your property for the purpose of applying Flying Stars Feng Shui.